A Bride's Book *of* Wedding Traditions

# A
# Bride's Book
## of
# Wedding
# Traditions

Arlene Hamilton Stewart

HEARST BOOKS

New York

Library of Congress Cataloging-in-Publication Data

Stewart, Arlene.
    A bride's book of wedding traditions / Arlene Hamilton Stewart.
      p.  cm.
    Includes index.
    ISBN 0–688–12768–1
    1. Wedding etiquette.  2. Weddings–Planning.  I. Title.
BJ2051.S7  1995
395'.22–dc20                                   94–39521
                                             CIP

Printed in the United States of America

5  6  7  8  9  10

BOOK DESIGN BY NINA OVRYN

For my sister *Ella*

# Acknowledgments

❧

Weddings are among life's most affirmative events, and that makes writing a book like this a pleasure. I am grateful to all who enriched this experience by sharing stories and traditions from their own weddings. In particular, I wish to thank my editor, Toni Sciarra, whose wonderful spirit and happy marriage provided the spark of creation for this work.

I could not have done the research involved without the assistance of the staff at the Katonah Public Library. Many thanks for their patience and interest. A special note of thanks goes to Sarah Stewart for her good-humored help.

# Contents

# Contents

*Chapter Three:*

## THE WEDDING RING 49

*Chapter Four:*

## PREPARING FOR THE WEDDING 67

# Contents

Contents

Contents

Contents

A Bride's Book *of* Wedding Traditions

# Before You Begin This Book

**W**hat is it that is so compelling about weddings? Nearly every bride-to-be becomes obsessed with her wedding, whether it takes place in a cathedral with six hundred guests, or on a hilltop with four. Is it because a wedding is a new beginning that every detail assumes fascination and importance? Or is it because of love— that extraordinary feeling for which we all long, and which we celebrate when declared publicly? It's hard to say exactly why we are so drawn to weddings, but since we are, let's admit it and find ways to savor every single moment of this fairy-tale-come-true experience.

One way is through tradition. "Tradition" doesn't mean wearing a conservative wedding dress with pearls or having four identically dressed bridesmaids. Wedding tradition is much more than that. Every wedding is a story of its own, much of it composed of traditions from the past that have been so absorbed into our expectations that they're almost invisible. As you plan your wedding, you will draw upon your memories of other weddings, your knowledge of what went before. It's amazing how innate that knowledge is, how much a part it is of our collective awareness. Any schoolgirl will emphatically inform you that brides wear white, should carry "something old, something new..."—and can never have too many flower girls and junior bridesmaids.

It's tradition that imbues celebrations with extra meaning, and no celebration is so endowed with tradition as a wedding. From the first thrilling moment of the engagement to the romantic return from the honeymoon, weddings overflow with centuries of continuing custom. Even when we look all the way back to the earliest weddings—which were the less-than-romantic "marriage by capture"—we find customs still in use today. Through wars, through social upheaval, and through sweeping technological changes, wedding traditions have remained surprisingly intact. For you, the bride, tradition resonates in every flower of your bouquet, every detail of your wedding ensemble. Your veil, your jewelry, even the color of your engagement ring all have deep meaning. You may not know why brides place a silver coin in their shoes, or why it's important to have the first slice of wedding cake, but you do it, as millions of other brides have done before you.

When we look beyond the happy whirl of wedding trimmings and traditions, the underlying truth of marriage is revealed. You are marrying for love, but throughout history, marriage also has served a broader purpose. It is nothing less than the steadying force that has ensured the continuation of society. From the beginning of time, our primitive ancestors bonded together. At the mercy of nature, they had no choice but to do so, and as they did, their clans and communities grew stronger. But they never took good fortune for granted; when they married, they made gestures of thanksgiving and appropriation to their gods. Grains thrown at the couple symbolized the wish for fertility, good crops, and harvest; words spoken in sacred spaces expressed the hope for benevolence; and loud noises—such as the sound of bells or the tinkle of champagne glasses—drove away the "jealous spirits" always lurking about at times of change. While the first wedding traditions grew out of the need for protection, over the centuries, others were born of love: the first diamond wedding ring created over six hundred years ago by a duke for his love; the bridal "shower" with its gifts of generosity; and the now-classic all-white wedding ensemble worn by young Queen Victoria as she married the great love of her life.

As you read these pages, I hope that the illumination of traditions will both entertain you and enrich your wedding experience. After all the rice has been tossed and as the last rose petal floats to the ground, your new life begins. This is a particularly wonderful time for women to marry. More so than at any other point in the past, women select their husbands solely for love and affection. Gone are the days of dowries and marriage by purchase, replaced by marriage for love. Any of the customs and traditions herein that help celebrate and safeguard this love are time's gift to you.

Although marriage ceremonies are constantly being refined to reflect the mood and spirit of the times, a bounty of tradition remains that allows us to honor both our common heritage and our individual ethnic heritage. We may not all jump the broom as many African Americans are now doing in homage to their past, and as many medieval Welsh brides did, but we might if we thought it would endow our marriages with an extra degree of love. And as we prepare delicacies for the wedding table, we realize that we are recipients of traditions from many cultures, from many eras.

Among the rich feast of wedding traditions, you will discover customs religious and solemn, lighthearted and fun. At the center of each is the most wonderful gift of all—hope: the hope that your marriage will be blessed with good health, a fine harvest, and above all, long-lasting love. And if you should encounter an elephant on your way to the wedding, let him go first. It's a tradition.

*Chapter One*

# Engagements

EITHER SEX ALONE

IS HALF ITSELF, AND IN TRUE MARRIAGE LIES

NOT EQUAL, NOR UNEQUAL.

*Alfred, Lord Tennyson*

ongratulations! You're engaged! Get set for a great ride, because between the engagement and the wedding stretches a vast land of merry-making, its route filled with delight and surprise. Engagement parties, bridesmaids' teas, groom's parties, showers, rehearsal dinners, and more await you. The traditions of this period are among life's most festive, and it's a wise bride who savors the sweetness of every moment.

Many of these engagement traditions were spun centuries

ago, but it seems as though most of them were polished to a glowing luster during the late 1800s. Could there have been an epoch that relished the high romance of an engagement more than the love-besotted Victorians? Pushing engagement etiquette to a new summit, Victorian mothers and fathers whisked the happy couple on a highly chaperoned, fast-paced romp of theater parties, concerts, ladies' luncheons, supper parties, and church socials.

What was the purpose of all this activity? There were two main goals here: first, to allow the couple greater access to each other; and second, to prepare them to participate in society by introducing them to a wider circle of people. Our Victorian ancestors viewed marriage not only as a romantic ideal, but also as an acceptance of the greater responsibility of being community members. When a couple married, they gained greater stature, and with that stature came duty. To-day, the orientation to community has changed; people are a part of a much larger world. Even though many couples are already well established in a professional milieu, they may not be very involved in community life. Marriage does have a way of changing that, deepening the ties to both neighbors and family. And one way this process starts is with the happy whirl of engagement activities.

With all there is to do, it would seem as though one

*Grow old along with me! The best is yet to be . . .*

ROBERT BROWNING: *"Rabbi Ben Ezra"*

would need an interminable engagement period. How long should an engagement be, and how does one make time for all the traditional celebrations and get-togethers? There is obviously no set rule about it, but a perceptible connection seemed to exist between the financial status of the parties involved and the length of the engagement. The wealthier the participants, the shorter the engagement. For well-to-do Victorians, three months was the norm. Since a wedding was regarded as the highlight of a young lady's social life, time was needed to collect wedding finery, shop for a trousseau, and tend to all the details of the ceremony and reception.

For many men and women in the past, however, especially those from working-class backgrounds, longer engagements were common. Month after month, the thrifty couple carefully saved enough capital and goods to set up their own home. This desire to be independent of in-laws is still a goal deeply ingrained in our social structure. In the 1800s and the decades preceding, it was not uncommon for men to marry when well into their thirties or older.

Today, many couples have a financial plan already in hand at the time they decide to marry, so for most, the main consideration is time—time to arrange the service, reception, flowers, clothes, and the million and one other matters that spring up. Most of this is determined by the degree of formality you want for your wedding. When setting your wedding date, you will find that the more formal the wedding, the more time will be required to make arrangements. Many popular reception sites are booked well in advance, as are orchestras, caterers, and wedding coordinators. This argues well for the at-home wedding, which many value as the most traditional wedding of all.

While today everything about an engagement should be joyful and positive, we have to face the historical reality that this was not always the case. Centuries ago, when betrothal was the forerunner to marriage, its character was dominated by business aspects. Prospective brides and grooms were merely instruments of a binding financial arrangement. As they waited in the wings for the formality of the marriage act, they could scarcely rhapsodize over the perfect spot for the bridesmaids' luncheon. But, true to the power of the wedding, even this unemotional time inspired traditions that remain recognizable today.

## · The Parents' Dinner ·

*T*he parents' dinner is a tradition that has stood the test of time. Soon after a couple decides to marry, a thrilling moment awaits them—telling their parents. In the not-so-distant past, it was the responsibility of the prospective groom to ask the bride's father for her hand in marriage. This gesture has nearly vanished in this country over the past twenty years. It has been replaced by a joint venture into breaking the news, most often to the bride's family first, a social nicety which may be appreciated—and remembered— by one's future in-laws.

After squeals of delight and tears of happiness, it's time to arrange one of the oldest of engagement rites: introducing one set of parents to the other. Traditionally, this ritual has taken place over the sharing of a meal. If no great distance separates the two families, the parents' dinner is still a charming idea, even if the couples are old friends who have known one another all their lives.

*The supreme happiness of life is the conviction we are loved.*

VICTOR HUGO:
*Les Misérables*

Breaking bread and eating together is one of the oldest customs uniting us. Far back in time, sharing the substance of life had deep meaning for people; an invitation to a meal was valued as a gift and tribute. At that time, all foods were prepared by the hosts. At an occasion as important as a marriage arrangement, tradition demanded only the best dishes. Evidence of this exists today, starting with a beautifully set table to underscore the extraordinary significance of the occasion. The table itself carries its own symbolic value, uniting what will become the new family around its welcoming perimeter.

Etiquette guides still advise the bride-to-be that hosting this get-together is the responsibility of the groom's parents. In Victorian days, soon after the news was made known to the parents, the groom's mother would call on the prospective bride and her mother, then issue an invitation to the bride's family for dinner. Time has altered this tradition. Many people live great distances apart, have hectic schedules, or are simply unaware of the protocol involved. Now it's a perfectly acceptable new custom for this special get-together to be hosted by either set of parents, or by the bridal couple themselves.

If ever there is a time to pull out all the stops, it's at this meal. What should one serve at such a momentous, yet intimate, event? Certainly a fine champagne or sparkling beverage contributes elegance and excitement. A glamorous, festive dessert, such as a trifle piled high with whipped cream, would be the perfect kickoff for the season of celebration about to follow. One way to heighten the intimacy of this occasion would be to serve beloved family delicacies as a way of getting to know each other better. This private dinner would usually start with a toast by the father of the groom or bride, before moving on to the inevitable: discussions of wedding plans, including ways to announce the engagement.

## ·The Engagement Party·

No matter how restrained they are, once parents are aware of this exhilarating news, they're usually bursting to share it with close friends and family. Here's where a phone service with good long-distance rates comes in handy. These calls have taken the place of formal, hand-written notes from the bride's mother which would announce the news to the family's closest relatives and friends. Note-writing is a gentle custom worthy of a revival, if for no other reason than that these missives make wonderful keepsakes for the family historian.

Many parents feel an engagement is such an important milestone in their children's lives that they wish to shout it from the rooftops. Instead, they gather their friends and family to share their happiness at the engagement party. This pleasing tradition allows everyone to rejoice in the engagement without the pressure of prescribed social forms. An engagement party can be anything from a late-night supper to a Sunday-morning picnic after church services. It can be a large crowd devouring Dad's waffles or a small circle of family and friends invited in for caviar and champagne. You might have a clambake on the beach, or dim sum in your favorite Chinese restaurant. Any party is fine, as long as it's buoyant and lighthearted.

One small note of caution: The engagement party is the first official recognition of your new status, so steel yourself for lots of questions about the wedding and your future. But don't worry; this is not a press conference. No mention need be made of your plans if you are not yet ready to do so. Remember, your engagement itself is a sufficiently thrilling reason to celebrate.

For centuries, the engagement party has been hosted by the parents of the bride. It took the twentieth century and our far-flung lifestyles to alter this custom, as well. Now, couples may elect to have this party hosted by a close friend or family member if their parents are not available. Many times, too, the groom's parents wish to participate in the party and may ask to share in the expenses. *Democracy* is the key word here. As an aside, it probably seems preposterous to point out that the guest list for the engagement party should include members of both the bride's and groom's families and circles of friends.

## · The Announcement ·

T he most dramatic moment of the party is, of course, the announcement. Who makes it? Since throughout most of history, female children have been regarded as their father's property, it's been customary for the father of the bride to do so. Nowadays, Dad's position is more sentimental than proprietal. He, or a high-ranking member of the family, simply asks for everyone's attention, and in a few simple words, expresses joy over the upcoming event. Time has liberalized this tradition, too. It's especially moving when a mother, sister, or good friend does these honors. In the absence of the bride's family, it's polite to request that a member of the groom's family make the announcement.

What about gifts at an engagement party? Is there a tradition for them? It should be pointed out that, unlike bridal showers, engagement parties are not recognized as automatic gift-giving occasions. Sometimes guests feel there is so much pressure on them to bring something "nice" to the party that they miss the point of the celebration—which is to share happiness with their loved ones. Only the closest friends and relatives should think of giving the bride something at the time of the announcement. If you receive gifts at the engagement party, perhaps you should open them afterward,

making sure to send a personal thank-you note the next day. Some couples like to take their guests by surprise with their thrilling news. This greatly heightens the excitement of the party, and has the added benefit of skirting the idea of gifts entirely.

## • The Newspaper Announcement •

N ow a high-powered status symbol in big-city news-papers, the published announcement has an old and honorable history. Up until the eighteenth century in Europe, before the printed invitation became commonplace, invitations to weddings were announced orally; that is, details of the wedding were shouted out by men hired to walk through villages informing the populace of the upcoming occasion. Two developments changed that: the growth of a larger, better-educated middle class, which in turn resulted in the popularity of newspapers. Soon, it became fashionable to have details of one's upcoming wedding announced in the paper. Later, as personal invitations became more widespread, this newspaper "invitation" evolved into the announcement of the impending nuptials.

If you want to announce your engagement in a local news-paper, contact the society desk. They'll let you know what

information is required. It's also interesting to note a brand-new tradition in the making regarding newspaper announcements: the photograph that features both the man and woman, rather than the woman alone. Unheard-of even ten years ago, more and more newspapers are printing joint photos of these two happy faces.

However you decide to announce your engagement—with a party, handwritten notes, telephone calls, or bush telegraph—remember to savor this precious period. Allow yourself time to reflect on all the wonderful things that are happening to you. Have a long brunch with your fiancé, and over a soothing cup of tea, share your thoughts, expectations, and all the funny things that have happened to you in your life together thus far. Now is the perfect moment to start a special wedding journal. After entering how you decided to marry, jot down the details of how you announced your wedding, and if you had a party, who attended, who made the toast, and so on. Even if you enter only a few lines, the journal will reward you with invaluable memories years later.

## · The Bridal Shower ·

Once the word is out about the wedding, the marriage machine really gets rolling. What other celebrations are in store? One of the interesting aspects of prewedding festivities is how they used to divide along gender lines. There are parties and celebrations that have been exclusively female, such as showers, and those that are all-male—the bachelor dinner or stag party. More and more of these divisions are blurring, but don't be surprised if you have at least one shower that is "for women only."

Even in the midst of profound social change between the sexes, the bridal shower is one wedding tradition that has never been threatened with extinction. With an ability to adapt that even a chameleon would admire, the bridal shower has reinvented itself in any number of socially and politically correct ways. For the feminist, there is the coed bridal shower attended, of course, by both men and women. For the conservation conscious, there is the "green" bridal shower, featuring earth-friendly home products. There is a world of choice in specialty showers: the linen shower for the nest-builder; the kitchen shower for the cook; the wine shower for *les amis du vin;* the tool shower for the home-improvement team. Not to mention the venerable lingerie shower, where a bride-to-be may be lucky enough to stock up on items she wouldn't have dared to buy for herself!

Since it seems irrefutable that the bridal shower will en-

*Never marry but for love, but see that thou lovest what is lovely.*

WILLIAM PENN:
*Some Fruits of Solitude*

dure as a tradition, it's interesting to look at its roots. What is the origin of this get-together? Wedding lore has it that the bridal shower dates back over three hundred years, when a young Dutch maiden fell in love with a poor miller, a man with a small fortune but a large heart. Because he often gave his flour to hungry families, he had no money to marry. The young lady's father refused to allow the marriage to take place without having his daughter properly set up. Seeing the girl's misery and knowing the miller's goodness, neighbors and friends figured out a way to provide her with enough household goods and furnishings to make a home. How? They gathered together and walked to the girl's house, each bringing a gift, and it seemed as though she were "showered" with gifts from heaven. This act of love so impressed the maiden's father that he gave his consent to the marriage.

Over time, this all-female party flourished as women showed support for one another. The gifts are the same as in the past—practical things to help start a new life—and the spirit is the same, too. As in the 1890s, guests may place their gifts in Japanese paper parasols to continue the "shower" motif, or tuck them in another popular Victorian container—the crepe paper wishing well. While the bride-to-be unwraps cooking utensils, tableware, and linens, hilarious jokes and stories fly. Women share valuable insights and secrets about the art of being married, and all bask in the warmth of sisterhood.

Who gives a bridal shower? Anyone who is close to the bride or groom may do so. Formerly, etiquette advisers would caution that the shower should not be hosted by a member of the bride's family, as it might appear too self-serving. Nowadays, this restriction, too, has been relaxed because of our busy lifestyles. Certainly, showers can be hosted by good friends of the couple, male or female.

Another variation of the bridal shower is the quilting bee. Quilting bees flourished in rural America throughout the early 1800s. In this charming and productive tradition, neighbors gathered together for an all-day event to sew a special wedding quilt for the bride and groom. Early in the morning, women took their places around a frame, where they would stitch together specially prepared sections, usually in the wedding-ring pattern or other traditional design. All day long busy hands would work, putting in stitch after careful stitch to make a quilt that would last a lifetime. After the quilt was finished, fiddles signaled the beginning of dancing, as an evening of well-earned festivity began.

# ·*The Bridesmaids' Tea*·

O nce the bride-to-be has selected her wedding attendants, she may want to consider holding a small
party to thank the dear friends and family who will be by
her side on the big day. Elegance is the sought-after char-
acteristic of this party, which in the past has been an afternoon tea or a small luncheon. And, while it's always the most
gracious to entertain at home, lunching at a favorite restaurant or bistro is an attractive option.

Since bridesmaids were such an important part of the wedding party in Victorian times, devoting much time and trouble to their many duties, the bride-to-be was lavish in her
thanks to them. In Great-Grandmother's day, out came the
best silver tea service, fine china, and fresh flowers. Lacy white
tablecloths were a backdrop for tiered dessert stands and
silver napkin rings, as petits fours, fruit tarts, lobster salad,
and watercress sandwiches were presented in all their glory.
Warm afternoon breezes would be caught on a veranda or
the buzz of honey-fat bees heard in the garden if the tea
took place in summer. Ice-cold fruit drinks poured in crystal
goblets punctuated the soothing heat. In winter, the fireside
or dining room would be the setting for a party as merry
and gay as the holiday season. Bracing soups and warm breads

would precede the grand finale—the "bridesmaids' cake." Made from flour sifted by the bride herself for good luck, this delectable creation was more than beautiful. It was as exciting as a visit to a fortune teller. For inside this special white-frosted layer cake the Victorian bride would have baked secret silver charms, each a talisman of wedding lore. As the bride sliced into the cake, her friends waited expectantly. One lucky maiden would receive a silver knot symbolizing the steadfastness of love. A heart promised romance, while a silver cat predicted an old maid! Whoever received a dime would receive fortune, and a silver wishbone portended good luck. Scissors implied busy hands, and the best charm of all, the silver ring, foretold the next to marry. With all this at stake, you might wonder: Could the bride tell where the charms were hidden? Tiny buttercream rosebuds or silver dragées was one way used to mark their location by a wily hostess.

The bridesmaids' tea is a lovely custom well worth the effort involved, because it brings you closer to your friends at this very emotional time. When the heat of the spotlight gets too intense, it's nice to be able to share it. Most brides like to hold this celebration shortly before the wedding, when emotions are running high. There are many ways to stage this delightful gathering besides the traditional at-home affair. The bridesmaids' tea need not be a tea at all. Brunch at a museum restaurant is wonderful; a picnic in a beautiful formal garden is a rare treat, as would be a visit to a beauty salon for a day of pampering. You may want to consider a car service to whisk you away to a vineyard, where you and your friends could sample fine wines and enjoy the pleasures of a slowly unfolding afternoon.

There is always a special moment when the bride-to-be brings forth her gifts for her bridesmaids. While the rehearsal dinner is the occasion when the bride and groom traditionally present members of the bridal party with special gifts and mementos, some brides prefer to use the bridesmaids' tea for this purpose, as it may be more private.

## · The Bachelor Party ·

*A*nd what about the groom during all this merry-making? He gets a party all his own, too, one that has also stood the test of time, though not without controversy: the bachelor dinner or stag party. Customarily, this all-male revelry takes place quite close to the actual wedding, as it has come to represent the groom's "last taste of freedom."

How did the bachelor dinner come about? It was supposed to have started in fifth-century Sparta, where military comrades would feast and toast one another on the eve of a wedding, much as they would salute a warrior gone down in battle. This bittersweet celebration does seem to possess an antifemale edge, especially in light of the risqué entertainment so often a part of the celebration. But others see this as a fun-filled tradition that allows the jittery groom and his wedding attendants to release some anxieties before the big day. It hardly needs pointing out that this decision is between the bride and groom. If either person has strong feelings about it, why not voice them diplomatically before any plans have been made?

## · B a n n s ·

D ating from the twelfth century, there is another custom still in practice in some countries today. Certainly, fans of early Agatha Christie mysteries always find themselves coming across mention of a couple's planning to wed, and before that happens, having the banns read in church. While not nearly as widespread as it once was, this custom is a direct descendant of the early English practice of announcing the couple's intention to marry publicly from the parish pulpit. It was thought that such a declaration would prevent any misunderstandings or fraud in the marriage agreement. Usually, banns are read at three successive services, to allow time for anyone objecting to voice his opinion.

## · B u n d l i n g ·

N o account of engagement traditions would be complete without a brief mention of the curious custom of bundling. Now an entirely discarded practice, bundling was a courting tradition in rural New England communities during the eighteenth century, brought to this country by settlers from Great Britain. How did a couple bundle? On a designated night, a courting couple was given permission to sleep in the same bed, but both were to wear underclothes. A long plank, or board, was set up between them which was supposed to remain in place during the night. It's not too hard to imagine that this was easier said than done, but it is interesting to know that nearly two centuries ago, unmarried young people were creative enough to find a way to sleep together under their parents' roof.

As we can see, the engagement period abounds with traditions that celebrate the important transitional state from single to married. More than anything, the engagement is a time of preparation as the two of you make hundreds of decisions about your ceremony, reception, honeymoon, and your new life afterward. Promise yourself that no matter how hectic it gets, you will keep a sense of humor about it. In that way, you guarantee that all your memories will be happy ones.

# Chapter Two

# Betrothal and Courtship: From Capture to Rapture

It is not good that

the man should be alone; I will

make him a help meet for him.

*Genesis 2.18*

eddings are the happiest of events. From that heart-pounding moment when you decide to marry, until you toast each other in your new home, weddings overflow with love. We like to think that love is immortal and has always been a part of our history, but this hasn't always been so. If we take a moment to look back in time, history reveals a vastly different heritage—that of women being married off as their families saw fit, most commonly for purposes of profit. For centuries, this practice prevailed over the existence of any tender feelings called *love*. It wasn't until the sixteenth century that the Elizabethans began to extol the virtues of love poetically, thus making romantic courtship at least an idea. Only in the past two hundred years has marrying for love turned into the rule, and not the exception. What an irony that today, in the United States, marrying "for money" is thought to be contemptible, yet this principle was the driving force behind marriage throughout most of history.

Nevertheless, even from the earliest days, weddings have generated sentimental traditions that have survived to our times: showers of rice; "Something old, something new . . ."; delicate bridal veils; and excited flower girls—these are only a few of the most beloved. As time passed, each civilization would make its own special contribution to wedding customs: the wedding cake from the Middle Ages; charming nosegays from the Elizabethans; and from the Victorians, the romance lexicons of flowers, fans, soulful looks. Even as wedding services are altered by each new generation, it's impressive how many wedding traditions have remained true to themselves—traditions that are so powerful that often couples follow them blindly without a clue as to their actual meaning.

## · *Tying the Knot* ·

W hen did weddings begin? Man was not put on earth in a tuxedo. How did our ancient brethren come together? If only Fred and Wilma Flintstone had left us a wedding album! It's difficult to say with certainty what prehistoric "marriages" were like. In the absence of banquet rooms and justices of the peace, more than likely, our primitive ancestors came together by living together. Some wedding historians imagine that men and women married by clasping hands or embracing in a space they considered sacred. Others think that primitive people may literally have "tied the knot" by lacing themselves together around the waists with reeds. This quaint custom springs up in many other later cultures in Holland, England, and Denmark when, on their wedding day, brides and grooms tied a ceremonious knot between themselves made of cord or ribbon.

It's hard to imagine the concept of love being celebrated thousands of years ago. Fear was most likely the most keenly felt emotion as early man struggled against floods, famine, lightning, and wild animals. Protection had more to do with men and women coming together than the desire to have a long, meaningful relationship. Practically all primitive people lived in tribes. Since loyalty to a tribe increased the chances of safety, many think the early forms of marriage were group marriages.

## · Candles at the Ceremony ·

**M**uch later in the course of civilization, the individual family emerged; and while allegiance to the tribe remained critical, coupling became the rule. Women had established their importance by bearing children, and we know that wherever there are women and children, there is shelter and food. Women literally kept the home fires burning while their men were out hunting or on raids.

Fire is one of the great forces of nature; without its sustaining warmth, there is no life—hence, fire has been worshiped from the earliest days. By the glow of candlelight, young Grecian girls were escorted to the altar. Roman brides were ceremoniously ushered to the hearth of their husbands' homes, the heart and soul of their new lives. Today, this tradition lives on in the brilliant flicker of candles placed upon altars and reception tables. As a bride, when you're arranging the candles for your reception, you will be tapping into a tradition thousands of years old. As you gaze at the variety of tapers, trying to select the perfect ones, perhaps for an antique candelabra, you may not realize it, but by that simple act, you are helping to ensure that your "home fires" will be a welcoming beacon over the lifetime of your marriage.

## ·Brides by Capture·

He took me in his strong white arms,
He bore me on his horse away,
O'er crag, morass, and hairbreadth pass,
But never asked me "Yea" or "Nay."

He made me fast with book and bell
With links of love he made me stay,
Till now I've neither heart, nor power,
Nor will, nor wish, to say him, "Nay."

*Christina Rossetti*

D espite the romance and ardor of this verse, in reality, marriage by capture could not have been too thrilling. Kidnapped either through tribal warfare, raids, or sheer cunning, the "bride" was forevermore the "groom's" property.

Tribal combat was an ongoing part of ancient life, however, and the spoils of war included women and children. Those seized from other tribes were exceptionally prized. Not only were they a symbol of victory over enemies; they were used as "fresh blood" for propagation purposes. Many ancient tribes had taboos against incest and close intermarriage, so it was extra-desirable to mate with a woman from outside the tribe.

## • Pretty Old Shoes •

*For this thou shalt*
*from all things seek,*
*Marrow of mirth and*
*laughter,*
*And wheresoe'ver thou*
*move, good luck*
*Shall throw her old*
*shoe after.*

ALFRED, LORD TENNYSON:
*"Lyrical Monologue"*

Oddly enough, the custom of tying old shoes to the bumpers of the bridal carriage is credited to the violent practice of marriage by capture. History has it that fathers of the abducted "brides" were so outraged by the kidnappings that they hurled their shoes in protest at the villainous rogues who had snatched their daughters. A more benign interpretation of this old custom is that shoes represented authority in ancient times. He who was wealthy enough to possess shoes was worthy of respect. It became a custom for the father of the bride to hand over a pair of shoes with his daughter, thereby transferring sovereignty over her to the husband.

## • Marriage by Purchase •

Given the prestige of adding an outsider to the clan, marriage by purchase was perhaps inevitable, for whenever someone possesses something that is of value to another, a form of currency will change hands.

There was no question that female children were the property of their fathers. When it came time for marital arrangements to be made, the bride's family was free to do so without her consent. Unmarried women could become financial burdens to a family in later years, and every effort was made to marry them off. This may have been the origin of the twin fears of dependency and spinsterhood that still haunt the female psyche, driving women into matches that are not ultimately in their self-interest. Marriage was the only way to escape the yoke of their fathers; sadly, even though a husband's yoke may have been lighter and of better quality, it was still a yoke.

## · Taking the Husband's Name ·

As the bride left her father's home, she also left behind his name. Assuming the name of her husband, she was recognized as his property. This most ancient tradition of taking the husband's name is alive and well today, adapted to any number of circumstances. Many brides return to this tradition as part of the nostalgia for simpler times. There are many other choices: retaining your birth name, hyphenated last names, with the bride's name last or first, or a whole new last name for the couple. It's an issue most brides resolve by themselves today, trying to decide among what is for some an uncomfortable historical reality, family solidarity, and the simple aesthetic of desiring a beautiful-sounding last name.

## •Betrothal•

*A*s weddings solidified into business transactions, the formal agreement to marry came to be known as the betrothal. Far from being a romantic engagement, the betrothal specified an exchange of goods and the date by which the marriage should be performed. Conducted before witnesses who could testify to its authenticity should a dispute arise, the betrothal was more significant than the wedding itself, because it signified agreement to the financial terms of the union. The betrothal ceremony took place at the conclusion of successful negotiations. Then followed a period when the bride-to-be and the groom could scrutinize each other more closely before the actual wedding, but they could not back out, because a betrothal was binding.

# ·Betrothal Ring·

*A*s romantic as it is to think that love has always been the motivating force behind marriage, history clearly reveals it was not. We have seen that most weddings were property transactions called betrothals. The bride and her dowry were on one side; the groom was on the other. As part of the ceremony, he was required to show good faith with a betrothal ring.

What were these early betrothal rings like? They were plain and primitive, although, even in those days, some were set with gemstones. Gold was popular with the aesthetically minded Egyptians; iron, with the practical Romans, who sometimes attached keys to the household stores to betrothal rings or pledge rings as testimony to the wife's trustworthiness and newly elevated social status. Of course, this ring would be too impractical to wear, so some Roman wives sported a fancy ring instead on public occasions. Many married women continue this tradition today, wearing their gold bands at home and saving the showy engagement ring for social occasions.

Most betrothal rings remained simple until about the eighth century, when Jewish jewelry makers created the most extraordinary designs. Shimmering in gold, these were towering edifices—representations of temples, often one or two inches high, or intricate boxes studded with precious gemstones, which could be used to hold something valuable. Though the workmanship was glorious, unfortunately, many of the rings were too bulky and impractical to actually wear, serving only a ceremonial purpose.

It was about this time that one of the greatest wedding traditions of all came into prominence: the plain gold wedding band. When brides look at trays of rings in jewelry shops today, they are not too different from brides in the eighth century visiting a jewelry maker. It was then that most European Christians were married with gold bands after having reached a betrothal agreement.

As marriage came under control of the Church in the sixteenth century, a wedding was not deemed official unless the bride was given a ring. Resourceful priests kept a supply on hand for the less-well-to-do brides and grooms to use during the ceremony. And ever since the Church established its domain, the ring has remained the most consistent wedding tradition, wavering only during the period of the Puritans, who banned them altogether in the seventeenth century.

## · The Espousal Gifts ·

*S*oon, betrothal became the marriage mode of the day, with very specific laws and codes defining its substance. In ancient Roman ceremonies, the bridal couple was betrothed in a ceremony known as a *sponsalia*, where, in the presence of ten witnesses, a sacred pledge to marry was made. The man was then known as the *sponsus* and he gave the woman a ring. The woman, known as the *sponsa*, then gave him something like cloth or a toga. It's here that we might see the beginning of the tradition of the engaged couple exchanging gifts. Although it would be challenging to find a toga today, its equivalent can easily be seen in the silk dressing gowns and velvet slippers brides like to present to their beloved ones.

## · Whence the Word Wed ·

*T*he word *wedding* is itself of ancient origin, stemming from the Anglo-Saxon betrothal ceremony. The agreement to marry was named the *beweddung,* and the down payment the groom made for his wife was called the *wed* or the *bridewealth.* Over time, a ring came to symbolize the betrothal payment. Since the betrothal agreement was difficult to break, it became known as *wedlock*. Today, we see vestiges of this tradition in the engagement rings worn by brides-to-be.

## · You Must Remember This: ·<br>Why Newlyweds Kiss at<br>the End of the Ceremony

A t betrothal ceremonies, the agreement was finalized by acts that have descended to us nearly intact. The prospective bride and groom joined hands. Then the ring was slipped on the prospective bride's fourth finger, right hand. Later, at the actual wedding, it was transferred to the left hand. Then came a drink, and the all-important kiss. Long ago, a betrothal kiss exchanged in front of witnesses was worth its weight in gold because it, more than any other part of the betrothal, made the agreement binding. If the groom wanted to back out anytime after the kiss, he was liable to forfeit all that he had agreed to pay for the bride.

It was then the custom for the actual wedding to take place no longer than two years from the betrothal ceremony. During Old English wedding services, the couple would again hold hands, the groom transferring the betrothal ring to the bride's left ring finger with the words, "With this ring, I wed thee, and with this gold and silver I honor thee." The bride, arrayed in a veil, would wear her hair long and flowing for the last time. Long hair represented virgin youth. After the ceremony, it was to be worn up as befitted the status of a married woman.

## · W h y   I s   t h e   B r i d e   C a r r i e d · O v e r   t h e   T h r e s h o l d   o f H e r   N e w   H o m e ?

*T*his tradition is nearly two thousand years old. Fire played an important part of life in Roman times; indeed, the center of the home was the hearth, called the *focus* in Latin. Upon returning home, Roman fathers would first pay tribute to the hearth. A Roman bride was brought in front of the hearth in her new home. She was escorted around it three times in a ceremony marking her as belonging in her husband's family. What does this have to do with a threshold? So great was the concern for this ceremony that all precautions were taken that she not trip or fall on her way to the hearth, which would have been a terrible sign of impending bad luck in the marriage. Thus, the groom's willing arms reached out to carry his new wife safely over the threshold and deposit her in front of the hearth. This is a lovely, custodial gesture on the groom's part, and it deserves a secure place in the wedding canon of traditions.

## • ''I Plight Thee My Troth'' •

*E*ver wonder where these immortal words came from? They are taken from the Church of England's Book of Common Prayer. Troth plighting was another popular form of betrothal in the Middle Ages. The word, taken from the Old English *treowth*, means truth. Troth plighting was popular mostly with poorer folks who had little to exchange except promises. Here, in a public setting, a couple would pledge fidelity to each other as a way of becoming betrothed before the wedding.

What of a material nature was exchanged for a bride? Silver and gold coins, or their equivalent: land, horses, cattle, other livestock, weapons, household goods. Sometimes, if the groom was poor, he made the promise of future work. In the Bible, Genesis 29:20, we read how Jacob agreed to work for seven years for Rachel: "So Jacob served seven years for Rachel, and they seemed only a few days to him because of the love he had for her."

# ·Dowries·

LET HER BEAUTY BE HER WEDDING DOWER.

*William Shakespeare:*
TWO GENTLEMEN OF VERONA

*W*hy does Dad pay for the wedding? It traces back to the question: What did a bride have to exchange for a good husband? Property was usually more prized than beauty, and the size of a bride's dowry helped determine her value. Acting from both selfish and generous impulses, fathers gave their daughters substantial dowries to attract decent husbands. The larger the bride's dowry, the more position she could command as a wife. An old adage advised, "A little of my own is better than a great deal of another's."

The ancient Greeks thought dowries were essential for their daughters. Some fathers pledged as much as 10 percent of their wealth to this purpose. Dowries were usually considered the bride's property to help protect her and any offspring in case of misfortune. Thus, dowries gave a wife leverage in a marriage; a husband had more motivation to please a well-off wife than a poor one.

Twelfth-century dowries were made up of household

goods such as linens, cooking utensils, furnishings, blankets, carpets, and jewels. In Victorian times, a dowry was often replaced by a settlement, along with a substantial trousseau. What is the twentieth-century equivalent of this magnanimity? Until recently, it was a tradition for the bride's father to pay the entire expense of the wedding.

## · The Bride Price ·

*I chose my wife, as she did her wedding gown, not for a fine glossy surface, but such qualities as would wear well.*

OLIVER GOLDSMITH:
*The Vicar of Wakefield*

When the custom of betrothal began, the prospective groom had to agree to what was called the "bride price," exchanging property with the bride's father for her hand in marriage. Sometimes the bride was traded for something not too flattering, like a cow or a mule, but most of the time, it was for land or currency. And like most big purchases, the bride was paid for "on time."

Lacking credit cards, not everyone had the means to come up with a betrothal ring. In those cases, a coin would be broken in two, the man and the woman each keeping half. Today's love-obsessed teenagers might be interested to know that the "broken-heart" charm is a direct descendant of this long-ago custom.

# · *The Church and Marriage* ·

THE TIME APPROACH'D, TO CHURCH THE PARTIES WENT,

AT ONCE WITH CARNAL AND DEVOUT INTENT:

FORTH CAME THE PRIEST, AND BADE TH'OBEDIENT WIFE,

LIKE SARAH OR REBECCA, LEAD HER LIFE:

THEN PRAY'D THE POWERS THE FRUITFUL

   BED TO BLESS,

AND MADE ALL SURE ENOUGH WITH HOLINESS.

> *Geoffrey Chaucer:*
> CANTERBURY TALES, "THE
> MERCHANTE'S TALE"

When we imagine a wedding ceremony, most of us picture a setting inside a church or synagogue, light streaming through stained-glass windows, flowers bedecking the altar. That's why it's surprising to realize that only in the past four hundred years have the majority of weddings actually taken place inside a house of worship. Before the mid-1500s, couples were free to marry themselves, then to ask for a priest's blessing afterward if they so wished. Another flourishing custom was for weddings to be held on the church porch or front steps, with the priest often making details of the dowry public:

SHE WAS A WORTHY WOMAN
ALL HER LIFE,
HUSBANDS AT THE CHURCH
DOOR, SHE HAD FIVE.

*Geoffrey Chaucer:*
CANTERBURY TALES, "THE WIFE OF
BATH"

But the Church in Europe had long wished to control the act of marriage. Finally, in 1563, the Council of Trent declared that marriage was a sacrament. Weddings moved inside the church and were performed at the altar.

This was not a universally embraced notion. The constitution resulting from the French Revolution in 1791 declared that religious ceremonies were not enough to make a marriage valid, that a civil ceremony was also necessary. The Puritans who came to power in England during the sixteenth century had similar thoughts, declaring religious marriage invalid without a civil ceremony. Today, in America, the state still has control of marriage. It is a prerequisite that a marriage license be obtained before a ceremony can be performed.

# ·Advise and Consent:·
## The Maid of Honor

*A*s long ago as the eleventh century, the notion that a bride would consent to her marriage, even an arranged one, gave weddings a new key player: the maid of honor. Once it was determined that women had the right to agree to their marriages, then two reliable witnesses who would vouch for them were required to sign the wedding registry. What better person to represent the bride than a dear friend? Before long, the maid of honor developed into a significant presence, adding her beauty and benevolence to what was turning into more and more of a happy prospect for brides.

Now, when you choose your maid of honor to be by your side as you take your vows, you are connecting with this giant advance that women made centuries ago. Women's rights have evolved with glacial slowness, but the maid of honor's presence is a symbol of the freedom of consent women now enjoy. When you choose your maid of honor, knowing the full significance of this role can only add to the deep meaning of your wedding.

## ·Wooing and Winning: The· Golden Age of Courtship

*Those marriages generally abound most with love and constancy that are preceded by a long courtship.*

JOSEPH ADDISON

❧

*B*etrothal died out in eighteenth-century England after laws were passed that effectively ended its legal status. This had an enormously liberating effect on courtship. Now, either side could end an engagement without great financial loss. More thought could be given to choosing a partner for reasons of love.

Courtship bloomed into an art form; engagements were less binding. Broken engagements are never nice, but even after being engaged, if a couple felt marriage was unworkable, the arrangement could be ended without great hardship.

## ·Victorian Women Who· Loved Too Much

*W*hat effect did liberalizing marriage laws have upon women? They became the center of a man's attention, of their desires. Women were celebrated for their beauty, their charms, their loving natures. The nuances of romantic courtship grew at an astonishing pace, reaching a peak in the Victorian era when decoding love's messages amounted to something like a full-time job for marriage-obsessed young women. So great was their involvement in even the smallest aspect of love that many elements of their courtship took on an infinite complexity. The language of the flowers, fans, sweets, dance cards, and calling cards had to be understood by any gentleman caller hoping to make a favorable impression. A fan held in the right hand in front of the face said, "Come closer," while the left hand said the opposite. Ladies' magazines and books coached lovers in the intricacies of courtship—giving us the origin of today's flourishing self-help "relationships" book market.

## · The Proposal ·

*I*f most marriages before the 1800s were arranged unions, how did the romantic proposal evolve? Contrary to popular notion, the groom has not always fallen to his knee, confessing his love and devotion to an overjoyed maiden. As bethrothal went out of practice in the eighteenth century, more and more women voiced their romantic intentions, making the first move toward the altar. Certainly, if the hopeful bride had social stature, then she could do the bidding herself. A wonderful example of this appears in Queen Victoria's journal where, on October 15, 1839, she recounts how she proposed to her beloved Prince Albert of Saxe-Coburg-Gotha:

At about 1/2 p. 12, I sent for Albert; he came to the Closet where I was alone, and after a few minutes I said to him, that I thought he must be aware why I wished him to come here, and that it would make me too happy if he would consent to what I wished; we embraced each other over and over again, and he was so kind, so affectionate; Oh! to feel I was, and am, loved by such an Angel as Albert was too great delight to describe! he is perfection; perfection in every way—in beauty—in everything!

These are probably your feelings exactly as you're transported from the ecstasy of proposal to the thrill of engagement.

*Chapter Three*

# The Wedding Ring

AND AS THIS ROUND

IS NOWHERE FOUND

TO FLAW OR ELSE TO SEVER,

SO LET OUR LOVE

AS ENDLESS PROVE

AND PURE AS GOLD FOREVER.

*Robert Herrick:*
"A RING PRESENTED TO JULIA"

 ithout a doubt, the most sentimental piece of jewelry in the world is the wedding ring. Fashion is fickle, but the simple purpose and honesty of the wedding ring has guaranteed it a place as the most universally understood symbol of love. And what a symbol it is!

Pure, elegant, and precious. It is an eloquent round shape that testifies to a love without an end.

It can be anything from an inexpensive, plain round band to a sapphire-and-diamond heirloom from a family vault; the wedding ring's pledge is every bit as lasting for one as another.

Rich in lore and history, the wedding ring is the most ancient of marriage symbols. After the wedding ceremony, the bride (and groom) is instantly recognized as a married person because of the ring worn on the fourth finger, left hand.

Every civilization since the Egyptians has sealed the marriage agreement with a ring. In fact, in Egyptian hieroglyphics, the symbol representing eternity is a circle. What were rings like before the advent of Tiffany's and Cartier's? The earliest known rings were of braided grasses, hay, leather, bone, and ivory. Later, as metals became more a part of daily life, lumpy-looking rings were formed from iron, silver, and gold. But practically all rings reflected the means of those marrying.

Before the days of coinage, rings were used as currency. Made of gold or silver, they were used to seal a bargain. Indeed, the Hebrews, Greeks, and Romans literally sealed an agreement by dipping signet rings in wax and affixing their seals to documents. At other times, rings were used as a form of reward and as a vote of confidence.

> AND THE PHARAOH SAID UNTO JOSEPH, "SEE, I HAVE
> SET THEE OVER ALL THE LAND OF EGYPT." AND
> PHARAOH TOOK OFF HIS SIGNET RING FROM HIS HAND,
> AND PUT IT UPON JOSEPH'S HAND . . .
>
> *Genesis 41:41–42*

Some credit the ring's origin as part of the wedding pledge to have derived from the very ancient custom of two people making a binding pledge by joining hands inside a sacred space, such as would be created by a ring of stones or trees. Most of all, however, the ring became part of an agreement to marry, because as an object of value, it showed that the husband trusted his wife with his property.

## · *W h i c h   I s   t h e   R e a l* ·  *R i n g   F i n g e r ?*

*O*nce you recite your vows, you are married, no matter where you wear your ring. But the most consistent tradition is the fourth finger, left hand. It's been that way since the days of the Egyptians. Why? A popular explanation is that the Egyptians believed that a vein on the left hand, the *vena amoris*, ran from that finger to the heart. More prosaic, perhaps, in the theory that since most people are right-handed, the left hand gets less use, and so a ring worn on the left hand is less likely to be damaged. Still, rings were worn on the right hand by many Roman Catholics until the eighteenth century, and it remains a tradition today for many European women to do so.

Another historical explanation for the left-handed wedding-ring finger is that at many early Anglo-Saxon wedding ceremonies, before the supervision of a priest was required by Church law, the bride and groom performed their own ceremony. The groom would hold the ring over the bride's left thumb saying, "In the name of the Father," then continuing, "in the name of the Son," he would hold the ring over the index finger, "and in the name of the Holy Ghost," over the middle finger, and finally, slip the ring on the fourth or "ring" finger saying, "Amen."

One less palatable theory for our romantic appetites is that the left hand has always represented servitude, since the right hand was the sword hand used to fight off enemies. Only those possessing property would fight off an enemy, and the historical truth was that the bride was the property of the groom. To this end, some believed that the bride accepted

*Father, and wife, and gentlemen adieu
I will to Venice.
Sunday comes apace.
We will have rings and things and fine array
And kiss me, Kate, we will be married on
Sunday.*

WILLIAM SHAKESPEARE:
*The Taming of the Shrew*

her lesser status by wearing a ring on her left hand. Indeed, some refer to this as the "ball-and-chain" concept.

Probably, however, the most likely reason why the left hand has remained the tradition is that the English Prayer Book of 1549 specified it for both the bride and groom.

If you think you would like to break with tradition and wear your wedding ring on a different finger, be advised that nearly every finger has been used for this purpose in the past, and all are acceptable. It was a fleeting fashion for well-to-do Elizabethans to wear elaborate, jumbo-size wedding rings on their thumbs, presumably as an indication that a leisured lifestyle would include no jewelry-damaging housework

*With this ring I thee wed, with my body I thee worship, and with my worldly goods I thee endow.*

Book of Common Prayer

## ·*The Gimmal Ring*·

M ost of us are familiar with a ring that consists of two, three, or more hoops that can be detached or worn separately, or threaded together to make a whole. This ring style is centuries old. First popular in the sixteenth century, this design is called the gimmal ring from the Latin word *geminius,* or twin.

At the betrothal, or engagement, the bride-to-be took one hoop, the prospective groom another, and if a third was a part of the design, it would be protected by a faithful witness until the time of the wedding. At the wedding, the hoops were reunited into one ring and placed upon the bride's hand. Occasionally, the groom kept one hoop after the wedding. To some, this was the begining of the double-ring tradition.

Lovers so embraced the romantic notion of the gimmal ring that it became a part of everyday life, as attested to by the seventeenth-century romance poet Robert Herrick in his collected verse *Hesperides:*

THOU SENT'ST ME A TRUE LOVE KNOT,
BUT I RETURNED A RING OF JUMMALS TO IMPLY
THY LOVE HAD BUT ONE KNOT, MINE A TRIPLE-TYE.

## · *The Fede Ring* ·

*A* peep at a jeweler's tray will reveal another betrothal ring style from long ago still in existence today: the fede ring, named after the Roman word for faith. Originally noted in the early 1600s, in this charming design, two small gold hands encircle either side of the ring, meet in its center, and clasp. In a sweet variation, two hearts are united by a key.

Like the gimmal ring, some fede rings were detachable,

the bride and groom each treasuring one piece until married. A small heart lay hidden beneath the hands in other styles.

## · The Posie Ring ·

ABOUT A HOOP OF GOLD, A PALTRY RING
THAT SHE DID GIVE ME; WHOSE POSY WAS
FOR ALL THE WORLD LIKE CUTLER'S POETRY
UPON A KNIFE—"LOVE ME AND LEAVE ME NOT."

*William Shakespeare:*
THE MERCHANT OF VENICE

*I*f you are thinking of having your wedding ring inscribed but can't find the right words, you could take inspiration from the tradition of the posie ring. It has long been a custom to engrave rings; the oldest inscribed rings were found in the tombs of the Egyptians. Queen Victoria gave her groom, Prince Albert, a gold band inscribed with the date OCT. 15, 1839—the day she proposed to him.

To the poetry-loving Elizabethans, however, this custom could not go far enough. With the first stirrings of romantic love (as opposed to economic advantage) as a reason for marrying, love mottoes and poetic couplets known as poesies were etched on the inside or outside of the band. It is a testimony to the skill and eyesight of Elizabethan jewelers that so many words could be engraved on a small wedding band yet, somehow, even long sentiments were written. Typical poesies might include:

HONEUR ET JOYE
LOVE NEVER ENDS

YOU AND I WILL LOVERS DIE
OF ALL THE REST I LOVE THEE BEST

CONSTANCY AND HEAVEN ARE ROUND
AND IN THIS EMBLEM FOUND

BE TRUE TO ME AND I TO THEE

I AM YOURS,
I DO REJOICE IN THEE MY CHOICE

MY LOVE IS FIXED, I WILL NOT RANGE,
I LIKE MY CHOICE TOO WELL TO CHANGE

## · The Keeper Ring ·

When it became the custom for the bride to have both a betrothal ring and a wedding ring, the betrothal ring, much like today's engagement ring, was often the more valuable of the two. Set with rare gemstones or wrought in elaborate styles, the betrothal ring was an asset worth protecting. Soon, some inventive jeweler created the keeper ring to protect these rings. Usually a round gold band, it would be worn above the more valuable ring, thus giving an esteemed bride three rings with which to impress her friends. King George III of Great Britain was credited with being the first to establish this fashion when he presented one to Queen Charlotte in 1761. Hers was a simple row of diamonds. If you love jewelry, you may wish to quote this historical precedent to your fiancé as justification for your own keeper ring.

*There is no remedy for love but to love more.*

HENRY DAVID THOREAU

## · D i a m o n d s ·

*E*ver since their discovery in India over two thousand years ago, diamonds have been the most coveted of all gemstones. Rubies may be the color of the heart, sapphires the color of the heavens, but diamonds are the color of power. Hard, able to withstand fire, unmatched for their brilliance, diamonds were regarded by the ancients as the stone of courage, the stone of the gods.

Even in cultures lacking the tools and skills necessary to release all their fire, diamonds wove a spell of mythical proportions. To the celestial-minded Greeks, diamonds (or *adamas* in their language) were thought to be the tears of the gods. To the poetic Romans, *diamas* were splinters falling from heavenly stars. So powerful was their allure that wise medieval Italians considered them *pietra della reconciliazione,* or "peace between husband and wife."

As early as the fifteenth century, diamonds were a powerful part of betrothal negotiations. The first record of a diamond ring used in wedding ceremonies is said to date from the year 1477. It was then that Archduke Maximilian of Austria won the hand of Mary of Burgundy with a gold-and-diamond ring. Large diamonds, cut in a style known as hogback, were fastened in a wide gold band that was elaborately engraved and ornamented with diamond baguettes.

However dazzling, the diamond ring remained out of reach for most except the wealthy until the discovery of the great South African diamond mines in the late nineteenth century. Still terribly expensive, the gems became more accessible to the middle classes as a variety of diamonds came on the market. Regarded (or rationalized) as an investment, diamonds are still, by far, the most desirable stones.

## • *Victorian Artistry* •

*I*f you love the beauty and grace of vintage jewelry and have always longed for an old-fashioned wedding ring, you are in luck. So prolific and inventive were the jewelry makers of the Victorian era that many wonderful rings can be found in antique shops today.

The Industrial Revolution of the nineteenth century created fortunes that needed to be spent. Whenever we find excess capital, we find a flourishing jewelry market. Jewelry was an instant status symbol, and Victorian jewelry makers stretched their talents to the limits by creating such charming designs that no bride-to-be could resist them. Twinkling from velvet trays were the new engagement-ring motifs. Foremost among them were hearts: the single heart, the double heart, the interlocking heart, hearts with crowns, hearts with locks and keys. Or the bride could choose a ring with gold made into knots, horseshoes, or a menagerie of exotic animals such as tigers and leopards.

But it was Queen Victoria, royal style setter and jewelry fancier, who opened the doors to new designs with her wedding ring—a gold coiled serpent (a symbol of eternity) with flashing diamond eyes. A creation of the court jeweler, Garrard, this spearheaded the trend for unusual wedding rings.

To the fanciful Victorian imagination, gold was the metal of the sun, silver of the moon, platinum of heaven. Gold remained the mainstay of the Victorian jewelry smith until the late nineteenth century, when platinum became more available. Platinum, because of its hardness, allows more intricate settings to be created, and thus, the fanciful styles we so associate with the turn of the century burst into bloom.

## · R e g a r d   R i n g s ·

*T*he Victorians were so infatuated with romantic symbols that nothing escaped a chance to be a part of their huge vocabulary of love—especially, the wedding ring. If you were a Victorian bride-to-be, you might be having a regard ring made up now. This was a ring with a message or sentiment spelled out by the first letter of each gemstone set in the ring. The name Mary, for instance, could be a cluster of <u>M</u>oonstone, <u>A</u>quamarine, <u>R</u>uby, and <u>Y</u>ellow diamonds. The word *regard* itself was often spelled out by <u>R</u>uby, <u>E</u>merald, <u>G</u>arnet, <u>A</u>quamarine, <u>R</u>uby, and <u>D</u>iamond.

When Queen Victoria's eldest son and heir to the throne, Albert Edward, was married in 1863, he gave his bride, Princess Alexandra of Denmark, a regard ring spelling her favorite nickname for him, Bertie: <u>B</u>eryl, <u>E</u>merald, <u>R</u>uby, <u>T</u>urquoise, <u>I</u>acynth, and <u>E</u>merald. As a generous touch, Bertie had the jeweler add a diamond to the ring to represent his bride.

## • G e m s t o n e s •

*I*n addition to their spectacular beauty, colored gemstones are prized as symbols of mystical power. The virtues bestowed upon gemstones delighted the knowledgeable Victorian lady and formed a part of her wedding strategy. If she wished to guarantee marital happiness, then a sapphire would have been her choice. To remain best friends with her husband, the bride would select a garnet. She knew that aquamarines brought out the intelligence of the wearer. And diamonds would protect against evil spirits. The ruby's brilliant flame was a protective shield. Emeralds were good for the eyes (although it was not always good for a wife to see everything!). Amethyst was a safeguard against drunkenness and was a favorite among early Roman wives. Until the eighteenth century, the opal was believed to be the luckiest of all stones. Coral is said to possess healing powers, but pearls, so beloved by brides today, were avoided, because their smooth teardrop shape reminded many of real tears.

## • B i r t h s t o n e s •

*A*round the turn of the century, a vogue came into being for setting birthstones in engagement rings.

Considered to have potent powers for those born in the designated month, the bridal birthstone could be either the groom's or the bride's.

Birthstones are beautiful gems in themselves, and they greatly expand a bride's options. They also fit in nicely with today's heightened interest in gemstones. If you are contemplating a birthstone engagement ring, here are the most commonly ascribed combinations:

| | |
|---|---|
| January | garnet |
| February | amethyst |
| March | aquamarine |
| April | diamond |
| May | emerald |
| June | pearl/agate |
| July | ruby |
| August | peridot |
| September | sapphire |
| October | opal |
| November | topaz |
| December | turquoise |

## ·*Shapes of Gemstones*·

*T*he quality of gemstones is composed of more than romantic legend and superstition; size, clarity, and cut are all important. Before the advent of precision cutting tools, gemstones were used in their natural state. One reason thought for the diamond's supremacy was that the uncut diamond can resemble a twin pyramid, that ancient symbol of power.

Toward the end of the fifteenth century, we saw the first cut-gemstone shapes made possible with a table saw. Rudimentary compared with today's complex faceting, these early gemstone engagement rings were still considered desirable. Later, as artistry developed, so did different cuts.

The elliptical cut was given the more elegant name of the *marquise* cut after Louis XV's mistress, Madame de Pompadour, who was a marquise. She had a particular liking for stones in this shape and had the means to have them provided for her. Also popular were pear-shaped gems, squares, and hearts.

*None love but they who wish to love.*

JEAN RACINE:
*Britannicus*

## ·*The Tiffany Solitaire*·

*"I*t's the new setting: of course it shows the stone beautifully, but it looks a little bare to old-

fashioned eyes," wrote Edith Wharton in *The Age of Innocence*, perhaps referring to the latest Tiffany setting style.

Of all the stone cuts and ring settings, there is one style that has reigned supreme for over a century: the diamond cut into the solitaire shape, then set into a mount pioneered by Tiffany's. Designed in the 1870s, this setting revolutionized the way brides saw their wedding rings. Up to that time, the setting was paramount, and the artistry of the jewelry maker was critical to its success. As diamonds grew in popularity and accessibility, their cuts had become more dazzling and complex. Now it was time to showcase the stone. The simple, six-prong Tiffany setting lifted the diamond high off its base allowing brilliant light to burst from the stone. Eye-catching and appealing, the gem was of greater importance than the setting, and brides loved it. They still love it. The Tiffany ring is probably the most universally known ring today.

## · The Groom's Ring ·

*A*lthough gifts of jewelry have always been exchanged by courting couples, historically men have chosen not to wear wedding rings. It was not until the sixteenth century, when they would split a gimmal ring with their betrothed, that they began to embrace the idea of wearing one.

However, as a symbol of a shared love and a commitment to equality in a marriage, the double-ring ceremony has gained in importance in this century, especially after World War II. Today, it is commonplace to see men wearing a larger version of the bride's wedding band.

## · Wedding Ring Superstitions ·

There are almost as many superstitions surrounding wedding rings as there are styles. A superstitious bride-to-be will not go ring shopping on a Friday, lest the bad luck of that day should rub off. Equally important is to avoid wearing a wedding ring before the ceremony, lest the gods should consider that presumptuous. Whatever you do, don't lose it or drop it during the ceremony, then you have to go back up the aisle and start the whole proceeding over! And—bad news for the antique fancier—don't buy someone else's ring, unless you know that marriage was supremely happy. The same holds true for those cherished family heirlooms.

# Chapter Four

# Preparing
# for the Wedding

PLANS GET YOU INTO THINGS...
BUT YOU GOT TO WORK YOUR WAY OUT.

*Will Rogers*

 early all couples are defenseless against the "wedding plan growth phenomenon." Most often, the
first thing to change is the size of the guest list.
The wedding list initially may include only the closest family
and friends. Then the names of important business associates
spring up, and those of Mother's bridge group. (After all,
she's attended *their* children's weddings for years!) The guest
list swells until your intimate afternoon ceremony has grown
into a breakfast with two hundred of your closest friends.

Weddings are highly emotional times when plans change constantly. We've come a long way since the days of betrothal, when a wedding was an economic transaction. We've even come a long way in the past twenty-five years, when it was still commonplace for the bride's parents to act as the sole "hosts" of a wedding. Today, weddings are more democratic. Brides and grooms share in making decisions and often in financial responsibility as well.

Before the pragmatic elements of plan-making come into play, take some time to determine the character of your wedding. Consider the mood, style, and degree of formality. Do you envision an affectionate family celebration with dancing and songs, or a more formal ceremony with a high degree of refinement? An exciting way to celebrate today is with a service that interweaves ethnic rituals from your heritage, such as a Shinto wedding or an African-American celebration.

## · The Three Types of Weddings ·

B asically, weddings fall into three categories: formal, semiformal, and informal. Remember, elements of one can be picked up and intertwined with another.

Tradition defines the formal wedding as one with a large guest list, usually two hundred or more. Other characteristics include: engraved invitations, a ceremony held in a large space such as a cathedral, synagogue, or grand ballroom, or outdoors in a splendid formal garden. Typical reception sites include hotels or clubs with formal rooms, or an estate.

Offering your guests a multicourse sit-down meal or lavish buffet is appropriate. The entire wedding party, including the mothers, dress in formal clothes; long gowns for women, cutaways for men. This type of wedding gives the bride the most fashion options—the most formal being a floor-length gown with a flowing veil and train. Flower girls, ring bearers, and pages are correct here. Bridesmaids may be included up to a dozen, and even more than twelve is not unusual in a formal wedding. The number is certainly up to the bride. It's noteworthy that in 1906, when Theodore Roosevelt's daughter, Alice, married in the White House in front of six hundred guests, she had no bridesmaids. When Lady Elizabeth Bowes-Lyon, the mother of present-day Queen Elizabeth II, married the duke of York in 1923, she was attended by eight bridesmaids.

For the formal wedding reception, live music played by an orchestra would serenade you. The entire affair would be decorated with an extravagance of arranged flowers.

A semiformal event bridges formal and informal weddings, and is a perfect choice when you have a large number of people to invite but don't want to be too elaborate. You might easily have seventy-five or more guests. Printed, engraved, or handwritten invitations are all suitable. A church, synagogue, or chapel would be the religious setting for the vows—or a spacious family home for a more personal service. A reception follows at a hotel, club, favorite restaurant, or at home. Guests are offered a buffet or sit-down meal. The bride is surrounded by as many attendants as she wishes, though a maid of honor and two or three bridesmaids is an accepted number, along with flower girl and ring bearer. For the bride, a long white gown with the option of a veil is one fashion direction; equally becoming and suitable would be a shorter dress of elegant line and color.

*Marriage is the perfection which love aimed at, ignorant of what it sought.*

RALPH WALDO EMERSON

As for the informal wedding, don't be misled by its name. This wedding can be just as elegant as a costly celebration for two hundred, and certainly just as momentous. In many respects, the informal wedding is the most traditional of all: until the beginning of this century, most weddings or receptions were held at the home of the bride's parents.

The guest list for an informal wedding is more modest, usually under seventy-five. Because of its size, you have the alternative of issuing handwritten invitations; an especially lovely option would be calligraphic invitations. This type of wedding feels best in a smaller, cozier setting such as the chapel of your hometown church, the book-lined study of a local judge, or in a garden blooming with June roses—which would also be an appealing site for the reception to follow. Refreshments are anything from light cocktail fare to a catered buffet. A selection of favorite family recipes is especially delightful at a small gathering. In the past, bridal attendants would have been limited to a few, but today, you might include as many as you like. As for the bride's ensemble, she would look charming in a dress or gown that is simple and unaffected; linens, silks, and cottons are always lovely. Family heirlooms are often preferred at this type of wedding, with shawls, veils, cameos, pearls, and family Bibles being among the most beloved.

Whatever your choice, your wedding bears the stamp of your personality, and it will be a symbol of your hopes for the future. There are some wonderful traditions that illuminate the way—some serious, some lighthearted. From the style of your invitations to the day, hour, and place of your wedding, you can pick up the strands of what you like and weave them into your own wedding tapestry.

## · When to Wed ·

MY BELOVED SPOKE, AND SAID UNTO ME:
"RISE UP, MY LOVE, MY FAIR ONE, AND COME AWAY.
FOR, LO, THE WINTER IS PAST,

THE RAIN IS OVER AND GONE;

THE FLOWERS APPEAR ON THE EARTH;

THE TIME OF SINGING IS COME,

AND THE VOICE OF THE TURTLE IS HEARD IN OUR LAND;

THE FIG-TREE PUTTETH FORTH HER GREEN FIGS,

AND THE VINES IN BLOSSOM GIVE FORTH THEIR FRAGRANCE.

ARISE, MY LOVE, MY FAIR ONE, AND COME AWAY."

*The Song of Songs*
*(Song of Solomon) 2:10–14*

*E*veryone agrees that weddings are exciting, whether it's your first or a remarriage. But, before you have your invitations printed, there are still so many decisions to make. You wonder: Where should the ceremony take place? What time? Why is June so popular for weddings? Fortunately, tradition has endowed us with a bounty of guidelines, superstitions, and folklore to help us make our choices.

## · S e t t i n g  t h e  D a t e ·

CHOOSE NOT ALONE A PROPER MATE,

BUT A PROPER TIME TO MARRY.

*Old folk saying*

*T*o our ancestors, the choice of the date of the marriage was meaningful. Every aspect of a wedding had significance. The day, hour, and particularly, the month were weighed and measured in the tales of folklore—as you can see from the famous English rhymes that follow.

## · J a n u a r y ·

MARRIED WHEN THE YEAR IS NEW,
HE'LL BE LOVING, KIND, AND TRUE.

To the ancient Greeks, January was the premiere wedding month. Why? It was dedicated to the powerful goddess Hera, wife of Zeus. Hera was the defender of women, and those who married during this month were thought to inherit an extra blessing. The ancient Romans carried out fertility rites during January, endowing the month with an additional benefit. And, of course, January has always been the month of new beginnings. If you are of Scottish ancestry, you would probably find January 1 the most fortuitous day to marry, as this day is regarded as extra lucky for any new endeavors.

# · *February* ·

WHEN FEBRUARY BIRDS DO MATE,
YOU WED NOR DREAD YOUR FATE.

O ver the centuries, the Church in Europe frowned upon weddings held during Lent, the period straddling the months of February and March. As the Church was able to exert its increasing influence, many marriages did not take place at this solemn time of year. This prohibition lasted through the nineteenth century. One notable exception was made for Queen Victoria, who had received complaints that the Church of England was dissatisfied with the Lenten time date set for the wedding of Prince Albert, her eldest son and heir to the British throne. The queen, who was also the titular head of the Church of England, replied with an economy of words, stating that marriage was "a solemn holy act, not to be classed with amusements." Prince Albert married Princess Alexandra on March 10, 1863, as planned. The queen herself was another February bride. She married Prince Albert on Monday, February 10, 1840.

## · March ·

IF YOU WED WHEN MARCH WINDS BLOW,

JOY AND SORROW BOTH YOU'LL KNOW.

*A*s the month is named for Mars, the Roman god of war, there was a sentiment that a March wedding could be inflicted with a belligerent quality. March also has the handicap of being a Lenten month. "Marry in Lent, you'll live to repent," is an old adage from the bucolic English countryside of the 1700s.

## · April ·

MARRY IN APRIL IF YOU CAN,

JOY FOR MAIDEN AND FOR MAN.

*H*and in hand with the cycles of the earth, the April wedding holds as much promise as the season. Since ancient times, this month has been deemed lucky for couples. April is the month held hallowed by Venus, the Roman goddess of love. In addition, many Romans married in the spring because homage was paid at that time to Ceres, the goddess of agriculture, and Flora, the goddess of flowers.

To the ancient Chinese, there could be no more pleasing time to marry than by the first flowering of delicate peach blossoms. Farming communities of long ago embraced the month of April, as it preceded the heavy demands of planting and harvest. In the southern part of our own country, April is a alluring choice because of the blooming of beloved flowers, especially jasmine.

## · M a y ·

MARRY IN THE MONTH OF MAY,
AND YOU'LL SURELY RUE THE DAY.

S tarting with the ancient Romans, a disinclination to the May marriage sprang from the custom of observing the festival of Lemuria, or the Feast of the Dead, in May. In an attempt to appease departed souls, women were prohibited from bright dress, ornamentation, and cosmetics. Even bathing was prohibited. Not such a good time for a honeymoon! In the Middle Ages, it was a popular belief that anyone who married in May would suffer misfortune within a year. So abiding was this stigma that even Queen Victoria would not allow any of her royal offspring to marry in May.

## · J u n e ·

MARRY WHEN JUNE ROSES GROW,
OVER LAND AND SEA YOU'LL GO.

*T*he month of June is another matter. The celebrated notion of the June bride owes its popularity to the ancient
Romans. For June was dedicated to Juno, the goddess of
women, who would safeguard those married during that period.
As June is a month graced by an abundance of roses, its romance
has intertwined with that of weddings to produce an ever-
enduring image of loveliness. "Married in the month of June,
life will be one long honeymoon." And, if you gauge your June
marriage to a new or full moon, you'll be uncommonly lucky.

## · J u l y ·

THOSE WHO IN JULY DO WED,
MUST LABOR FOR THEIR DAILY BREAD.

"*M*arried in July with flowers ablaze, Bitter-sweet
memories in after days." From these folk
rhymes, we can see that July doesn't seem to be the most
exemplary month in which to marry. In rural communities,

farmers tried to avoid marrying between the time of hay and harvest, because boundless wedding feasts would keep laborers away from the fields.

## · A u g u s t ·

WHOEVER WED IN AUGUST BE,
MANY A CHANGE IS SURE TO SEE.

*A*ugust is the first month of harvest, and like July, it was not the time for weddings in farming communities. Apart from that, it seems to be a month relatively free of proprieties. Perhaps because of its proximity to one of nature's cycles, the August wedding possesses an air of late-summer maturity.

## · S e p t e m b e r ·

MARRY IN SEPTEMBER'S SHINE,
YOUR LIVING WILL BE RICH AND FINE.

*S*eptember's warmth and abundance has blessed many a marriage. Blazing autumn colors make a glorious backdrop for festivities. For centuries, the full harvest moon has been thought to enhance fertility and thus bless a union.

## · October ·

IF IN OCTOBER, YOU DO MARRY
LOVE WILL COME, BUT RICHES TARRY.

T he Victorians adored the October wedding with "leaves all golden and red." The appeal of a wedding was in perfect keeping with that of the season. But an earlier adage warned: "Married when leaves in October thin, Toil and hardships for you begin."

## · November ·

IF YOU WED IN BLEAK NOVEMBER,
ONLY JOYS WILL COME, REMEMBER.

P erhaps because everyone is so busy planning for the holidays, November has been a relatively unpopular month for weddings. Still, if one were to heed the advice above, it promises much good fortune. The ancient Greeks liked a wedding in the colder months, especially at the time of a full moon.

# ·December·

WHEN DECEMBER'S SNOWS FALL FAST,

MARRY, AND TRUE LOVE WILL LAST.

*T*he joys of this month have enriched many a wedding. With the glow of candlelight and the fragrance of Christmas greenery, few weddings are as romantic as the December wedding. This has been a traditional favorite for marriage as it combines the joy of the wedding with that of the holiday. Snow falling on a wedding day is thought to foretell happiness. An old Irish superstition makes the last day of the old year particularly fortuitous for weddings.

## ·Day of the Week·

MONDAY FOR WEALTH,

TUESDAY FOR HEALTH,

WEDNESDAY THE BEST DAY OF ALL.

THURSDAY FOR CROSSES,

FRIDAY FOR LOSSES,

SATURDAY, NO LUCK AT ALL.

*Old English folk rhyme*

*O*nce you decide the month of your marriage, then the day of the week becomes the next decision. While Saturday seems to be the traditional favorite, certainly among Christians, Sunday is the day most Jewish weddings take place (since Saturday is the Sabbath day of rest and prayer). The Saturday Christian observance is really an outgrowth of the concept of the work week and the evolution of the weekend. Perhaps the old folk rhyme above omits Sunday because for centuries, weddings were so commonly celebrated on Sundays. That was understandable, it being the only day of the week most laborers had off.

Unlike ordinary folk, royalty was free to exercise its own thoughts about marriage. Weddings were timed according to astrological advice, political objectives, dynastic purposes, or whim.

## · The Best Day of All to Marry ·

*T*he Victorians, ever curious about the "meanings" bred in social nuances, believed it was lucky to marry on the same day of the week as the groom was born. In fact, the best day of all to marry was on the groom's birthday.

## ·*What Time to Marry*·

"*H*appy the bride the sun shines on," says an old proverb. And indeed, long before the days of sunscreens, the sun was truly worshiped. Sunlight was essential for crops to grow. It illuminated all, providing warmth and comfort. A bride upon whom the sun would fall was thought to receive an extra measure of good fortune. We see this esteem for the sun in many cultures. For example, on their wedding day, Asian brides and grooms bow to the sun upon rising.

This desire to be blessed by the sun may account for the popularity of early-morning weddings. Getting an early start on the feasting was certainly another. In England, up until the late 1800s, Sunday was the day to marry—and before noon, in order to have a church service after the vows. Royalty had a tradition of marrying at night. Queen Victoria broke with this in 1840 when she held her service at one o'clock in the afternoon. On a more contemporary note, most etiquette guides advise an "early" ceremony. This can be anywhere from ten in the morning to late afternoon. The morning wedding has a practical dimension to it. After an early start, the newlyweds can squeeze in some travel time following the reception.

# · *Where to Wed: Sacred Spaces* ·

O nce you decide the day, time, and month, now all you have to do is decide where. Weddings were not always held in churches or synagogues. Nevertheless, throughout the ages, couples have sought to have their unions blessed by holding the ceremony in a sacred space. To our earliest ancestors, a sacred space was one created by nature. The site possessed a quality that personified the endless force of life, such as a tree venerated for its spirit and age, or a sacred stone with an opening through which a couple could marry by holding hands. One of the most sacred ancestral places is where earth meets heaven—a hilltop or a cliff top. Today, the top of a skyscraper is a modern interpretation of this locale.

Another powerful force of nature is fire. Reverence for fire played a large part in many ancient civilizations; fire sustained life and homage was paid to it. In ancient Greece, brides were led to a ceremony before the hearth, where they made offerings to the household gods. When today's bride marries at home in front of her fireplace, she is reenacting this tribute, and we hope she will reap an extra measure of good fortune.

Before the thirteenth century, many couples simply married themselves, or were married by elders after the betrothal agreement. Churches did not have control of weddings, so

*Oh happy state! when souls each other draw, When love is liberty, and nature, law.*

ALEXANDER POPE:
*"Eloisa to Abelard"*

many marriages took place outside the church—but not too far outside: the church steps or front porch became a popular site on which couples exchanged vows, under the auspices of the clergy. Later, the wedding moved into the church—or up to the altar, another "sacred space."

## · T h e  A t - H o m e  W e d d i n g ·

During the brief period of Puritan rule in England (1653–56), the Civil Marriage Act came into law. Justices of the peace were the only officials allowed to marry couples—and, frequently, these marriages took place in the bride's home. While Puritan rule may have been short-lived, its influence was far-reaching. In the America of our early settlers, many of whom were Puritans, the at-home wedding became firmly established. At the same time, another segment of the American population celebrated weddings at home, too. For example, Indian maidens from the Algonquin tribe were escorted to their bridegrooms' lodges on their wedding day.

Much as a gardener plants seeds in the spring taking into consideration elements of nature—the sun, weather, placement of plants—your wedding will blossom from your careful planning. Our ancestors listened to every nuance of nature.

Choosing the right things for yourself in terms of style, location, and timing can only heighten the beauty of your day. Seeing your celebration come into its own glory will be one of your rewards.

## · *The Invitation* ·

Suspend for one day, your cares and labors,

And come to the wedding, kind friends and good neighbors.

*Old English ditty*

O nce you decide on the type of wedding you want, consider how to invite your guests. For example, people living in parts of Africa would receive this glad news from a family friend, making his rounds with oral invitations. In the United States, the engraved invitation may seem to be the classic, but it's interesting to know there are other traditional options, too.

As with so many wedding traditions, the exact origin of the invitation is obscured by time. However, it is generally believed that in olden days of the English countryside, before the ability to read became widespread, invitations were shouted out by "bidders." These were old men hired to announce the details of the wedding. Since most early wedding celebrations were spirited community events, all who fell within earshot instantly became part of the sizable guest list. This form of invitation was commonplace for ordinary folk, and it endured until the eighteenth century, when invitations published in newspapers became popular.

When did the written invitation begin? Starting in the Middle Ages, wealthy folk—the gentry or nobility—were the first to have the means to purchase precious written invitations. Many were beautiful works of art, inscribed by monks. This tradition stemmed from the practice of monasteries maintaining records of royal marriages. Using the same exquisite script that illuminated much of their calligraphic works, the monks wrote out the invitations. Should you decide to have your invitations written in a calligraphic hand, not only are you creating a thing of beauty, you are also honoring one of the oldest wedding traditions.

At the same time that monks in European monasteries were toiling away with their calligraphic nibs, in North America, native Indian tribes were highly conversant with the art of the invitation. The hospitality of Native-American tribes is legendary. Smoke signals were their formal request, followed up by personalized inscriptions on birch bark.

## • *The Engraved Invitation* •

*I*n the early 1600s, copper plate engravings of script began to replace the time-consuming art of hand lettering. Thus the custom of the engraved invitation began. Typefaces such as antique roman, shaded roman, or fancy Gothic were actually replicas of the lettering penned by monks. Invitations were also printed in black ink to further duplicate the look of calligraphy.

The other popular form of printed invitations is thermography. In this process, the ink flows onto the paper, giving the invitations a raised texture. This is much less expensive than engraving, but it does lack the sharp profile of engraving. Technology changes tradition, and today, we have the newly emerging, yet socially unsanctioned, tradition of the invitation by facsimile machine. Of course, it takes a fax machine to receive a fax, so one is not totally defenseless— yet! A trend in the making is the computer-generated invitation designed by the bride and groom. This is certainly a way to personalize your invitation.

## ·*Deliver the Letter*·

*A*s part of their fascination with social forms, the Victorians considered a wedding of fifty or less to merit handwritten invitations. As charming as these invitations were, how did they reach the intended guests? Today, we take the postal service for granted. But this was not always so. Until this century, special letters were usually hand-delivered, either by a servant or courier. Why? In early Victorian days, the mail system was disparaged as unreliable and undistinguished. To entrust a message to its questionable service was to demean the missive's importance and to imply that the recipient was not worthy of a hand-delivered letter. In other words, a mailed invitation was in poor taste.

As mail service improved during the late 1800s, both in America and Europe, mailed invitations became the standard. Today, we have the reverse of this tradition. It is a lovely, if extravagant, gesture to have invitations hand-delivered. Given today's busy lifestyles and preoccupation with security, however, this custom seems headed for the fate of the calling card.

# · Wording, Packaging, ·
## and Timing

*T*he invitation is another part of the great semantic code of weddings. Its appearance, wording, and even its weight inform the guest as to the degree of formality of the service so that he may plan accordingly. A traditional engraved invitation with outer and inner envelopes and a sheet of tissue paper signals fancy dress and an elaborate reception afterward.

In the past, the wording for weddings was very prescribed, and the proprieties for this are enough to drive even an etiquette expert insane. For example, the father and mother of the bride requested the "honour" (note British spelling) of a guest's presence at a formal wedding, and the "pleasure" of a guest's presence at an informal wedding. Fortunately, today we are not so rulebound. Lifestyle changes have influenced weddings. There are many variations on wording. It's not unusual to see the names of both sets of parents as hosts on the invitation. There is a charming old Mexican tradition for guests to receive two identical invitations, one from the bride's family, one from the groom's.

If you're baffled by all the options, one approach is to visit your stationer. More than likely, you'll be shown a variety of phraseology styles that reflect today's changes. Take

*Love reckons hours for months, and days for years
And every little absence is an age.*

JOHN DRYDEN:
*Amphitryon*

❧

home some samples and think about how you want your invitation to read. Don't feel pressured into making a decision on the spot. Invitations are precious keepsakes, and it's important you get what you want.

# · R . S . V . P . ·

*I*nvitations are often accompanied by a smaller, formal reception card. Should you reverse the scheme of things and decide on a very grand reception with more guests than at the ceremony, you may make the reception card the more outstanding of the two. It is now an established custom to include a small R.S.V.P. card along with the invitation. Many guests feel they do not need to be reminded to reply to something as important as a wedding invitation, and may be miffed by the presence of this card. Certainly, a reply card affixed with a stamp would be rubbing it in to those who share this sensibility. Alternatively, other guests may regard the R.S.V.P. card as a convenience and be grateful for its inclusion. They can be most helpful when keeping a head count.

Invitations for semiformal weddings are engraved or printed on paper in any size or color. Cream or ivory stock is not the only color choice. Today, there is a profusion of beautiful handmade papers that make marvelous wedding invitations.

When are invitations sent out? The Victorians allowed as few as fifteen days before the wedding. This seems to be very short today, considering how full most people's social calendars are. The basic rationale is to allow enough time to receive replies—three or four weeks being the consensus among today's etiquette experts.

## · W h y   T w o   E n v e l o p e s ? ·

*T*he tradition of inserting one envelope into another underscores the dignity of the invitation: by making it less accessible, it becomes more valuable. Also, the inner envelope protects the precious contents from too much handling. Oddly enough, there can be a backlash against this seemingly innocent gesture. Many people deplore the waste of paper products and consider this wasteful. You can easily omit this extra envelope, should you agree.

Why a sheet of tissue paper? Most engraved or printed invitations arrive from the printer with a delicate sheet of paper inserted between each invitation. This nicety protects the print from smearing. So many brides like the look of the tissue that they leave it in with the invitation. Whether you do or not depends on your taste.

*Chapter Five*

# The Wedding Party

FULL MANY MAIDS CLAD IN THEIR BEST ARRAY,
IN HONOUR OF THE BRIDE, COME WITH THEIR FLASKETS,
FILL'D FULL OF FLOWERS, OTHERS IN WICKER BASKETS.

*William Browne:*
BRITANNIA'S PASTORAL

early every wedding album contains the classic
portrait of the wedding party. Lined up, side by
side with the bride and groom, smiling faces
look out at us reflecting the joy in their hearts. Splendid in
finery that most likely will be worn but once, the maid of
honor, best man, bridesmaids, ushers, flower girls, ring bearers, and the newlyweds' parents join with the bride and
groom as they take this momentous step. What forces have

brought this group together? And why is the tradition of the wedding party such an enduring one?

Going far back in antiquity, the first bridal attendants were not designated *bridesmaid, maid of honor,* or *flower girl;* they were more of an honor guard selected to escort the couple to the ceremony. Times of change or transition require protection. In ancient Greek civilization, marriage was serious. Weddings were sacred affairs conducted before the altars of the gods. Every endeavor was made to appease the great forces of nature that dominated their lives.

## · The First Bridesmaids ·

LADIES OF HONOR, WORTHY WIVES
OF WORTHY HUSBANDS, OLD IN LOVE
ESCORT HER IN...

*Gaius Valerius Catullus*

M ost Greek women were married at the age of fifteen. To steer this young, inexperienced person safely into marriage, a flotilla of older married women escorted her to the ceremony. Since much faith was placed in symbols, only women who had been happy and fertile in their own marriages were included. The underlying hope and strategy here was that the wisdom and good fortune of this womanly group would rub off on the bride. Assembling at her home, this escort surrounded the bride as she walked to the ceremony, protecting her from evil forces from the moment she left her old world until she entered her new.

Young children walked before the group, strewing grains and herbs in the bride's path as a tribute to the gods who could ensure her fertility. Later, in medieval times, the group of children became a pair of young girls who carried flowers mixed with grains and herbs. These busy children from long ago are easily recognizable antecedents to today's flower girls.

The custom of a bridal escort was also a part of the Roman rites of marriage. Patrician brides and grooms, elegant in flowing white robes, were accompanied to the altar by a group of ten witnesses, usually friends of the bride's family.

Another way Roman bridesmaids helped out was to carry large trays laden with the small "wedding cakes" shared by all after the ceremony.

## · Who Helped the Groom? ·

*E*ven in the primitive, preromance days of marriage by capture, when Anglo-Saxon tribesmen on horseback swept down on helpless maidens to steal them for marriage, the so-called groom was accompanied by comrades. Their mission was to make his raid successful and perhaps steal a "wife" of their own. These young groom's men were bold forerunners of today's more law-abiding ushers and best men.

How did maidens protect themselves from capture by these marauders? When outside the confines of the tribal village, they banded together. Unfortunately, when one young woman was captured, often another was as well. Later, we see groomsmen or "bride's knights" being dispatched by the groom to the home of the bride to ensure her safe passage to her new home.

TWO LUSTY LADS, WELL DREST AND STRONG,
STEP'D OUT TO HELP THE BRIDE ALONG;
AND TWO YOUNG MAIDS OF EQUAL SIZE,
AS SOON THE BRIDEGROOM'S HAND SUPRIZE.

*Edward Chicken:*
"THE COLLIER'S WEDDING"

So embedded in British wedding myth is this notion of chase and capture that centuries later, mock struggles were reenacted at the bride's door. The bride's friends, or brides-maids, feigned resistance on her behalf as the groom's friends pretended to invade her house. Over the years, gentler as-sociations have graced the bridesmaid's image. No longer required to physically protect her friend, the bridesmaid would henceforth protect her emotionally, sustaining her throughout the wedding preparations.

From the time of earliest civilization to today, friends have always surrounded the bride and groom—as the best man, maid of honor, and bridesmaid. And while some may think that these roles are purely honorary and sentimental, we shall see that there are meaningful services each bridal attendant provides—besides the most meaningful one of all—showing up and smiling.

## • The Maid of Honor •

"*A* friend is a present that you give yourself," wrote Ralph Waldo Emerson. When a woman marries, it's more than a blessing to have such a friend by her side. It's a necessity. There is so much to do, and so many decisions to make, and this happy but hectic time has always been more fun when shared with a friend.

As we've seen, the tradition of the bridal attendant is an old and honorable one graced with more than symbolic importance. From the late Middle Ages to the present, a marriage was not considered official unless witnessed by two people. Why? It's hard to believe it in this era of romantic love, but the restriction resulted from the practice of women being unwillingly married off by their fathers. The witnesses swore that the bride was entering into the match voluntarily; and one of these two witnesses was usually a friend of the bride's. She became known as the maid of honor.

Besides this important function, the maid of honor had other duties. During the Elizabethan era, at the same time that Shakespeare was eloquently describing the "marriage of true minds," the bride and her maid of honor spent many pleasant hours preparing for the wedding. For a late-summer wedding, they made dozens of tiny nosegays to give to the guests. Fashioned from rosemary, the herb renowned for inspiring loyalty, the nosegays were tied with bright ribbons into "love knots." During long winter afternoons, the bride and her friend spun yarns to weave into cloths for the bride's new home, or embroidered linens as part of her trousseau. At the reception, or feast, the maid of honor might have been asked to hold the "dow-purse" containing coins presented to the bride.

To Victorian ladies, it was a great honor to be asked to be a friend's maid of honor. Besides being publicly acknowledged as a great friend, there was hidden benefit to the role. Most Victorian brides dressed their wedding party in gowns as fine as their own; this created an automatic showcase for

*Love looks not with the eyes but with the mind, And therefore is winged Cupid painted blind.*

WILLIAM SHAKESPEARE:
*A Midsummer Night's Dream*

bridesmaids who would be particularly eye-catching to un-married males.

## ·Who Should Be the Maid· of Honor?

*I*n the past, as today, the traditional choice would have been the bride's sister or best friend. Should she already be married, her title was matron of honor. This gave the bride the option of including an unmarried lady as maid of honor. For us, in the post-Ms. era, these distinctions have blurred somewhat. If at your wedding you include two such special attendants, both may stand next to you at the altar, or wherever you choose to exchange your vows. One may hold your flowers; the other signs the bridal register.

## ·Maid of Honor's Duties·

*I*n the past, the maid of honor had much to do in the months and weeks before the wedding. Since few young women worked outside the home at the turn of the century, marriage for most was their "career goal." Time devoted to the pleasurable tasks surrounding a friend's wedding usually paid off, because a wedding enhanced a young woman's chances of meeting the man she would marry. Hours flew by fitting gowns, addressing invitations, making favours, and, most important, shopping for the bride's trousseau. In Victorian days, trousseaux were serious matters. Affluent brides departed for their new homes with "a dozen of everything," so this could involve many hours collecting household linens and furnishings, china, and enough clothes to last a lifetime.

The eve of the wedding would find the bride and her bridesmaids caught up in another happy tradition: the pre-wedding sleep-over. In order for them to assist with the important ritual of dressing the next day, custom decreed that bridesmaids sleep at the bride's house.

After ribbons were tied and laces flounced, the wedding party departed for the ceremony. Just before leaving, the resourceful maid of honor tucked an extra handkerchief, fan, even a small vial of smelling salts in her bag for emergencies.

Arriving at the ceremony, the maid of honor arranged the bride's veil into a heavenly array. Next, she checked that all the other attendants, especially the flower girls and ring bearers, were in the right place. Once the first notes of Mendelssohn's "Wedding March" were heard, all proceeded down the aisle, with the maid of honor taking her place just before the bride. If the bride wore a gown with a train, the maid of honor arranged it in a beautiful spill at the altar.

*O Bridesmaid, ere the happy knot was tied, Thine eyes as wept that they could hardly see; Thy sister smiled and said, "No tears for me! A happy bridesmaid makes a happy bride."*

ALFRED, LORD TENNYSON:

*"The Bridesmaid"*

She held the bride's bouquet when the bride received her ring and, in the case of a double-ring ceremony, safeguarded the groom's ring until the bride slipped it on his finger.

After all this attention to detail, one would think the maid of honor could relax at the reception, but her duties were not over yet. Soon it was time to slip away with the bride to help her dress for the wedding-trip departure. Once the wedding gown was safely tucked away and the last of the luggage packed, the maid of honor hastened back to the reception. It was time for the bridal bouquet toss.

The maid of honor's role has remained true to many of these traditions. While today she may be more of a sounding board for the bride than a tireless trousseau shopper, she still provides the invaluable gift of friendship as the bride sets out upon one of life's most exciting journeys.

## · The Bridesmaids ·

What a lovely tradition bridesmaids are! "Bridesmaids in waiting, gather now and lift harmonious voices," wrote Catullus in 60 B.C. Even that long ago, bridesmaids were celebrated for the happiness they brought to a wedding. Their roles, still mostly decorative, are completely charming. Who else would willingly dress up in identical

outfits which they will wear only once and will pay for themselves—and do it with such good grace? Who else is so
sweet-natured about dancing with the bride and groom's
relatives that they waltz off with everyone's hearts? Who else
is good-natured enough to make dozens of party favours and
line up eagerly to catch the bridal bouquet? It could only be
the bridesmaids.

Since days immemorial, women have helped one another
at life's significant turning points—weddings and childbirth
being the most notable. Just as the maid of honor helps the
bride, so do the bridesmaids. Their presence is comforting,
and despite a dearth of major duties, their participation is
still a prominent part of the celebration.

As long ago as the fifth century, English bridesmaids helped
to make wreaths for all members of the wedding party to wear.
In Elizabethan times, bridesmaids gathered before the wedding
feast to knot yards of rope with flowers, which they would
hang from arches and doorways. Bridesmaids also prepared a
special nosegay for the groom, one made of rosemary, the herb
thought to inspire loyalty. It was an early English custom for
bridesmaids to plant a sprig of myrtle, which symbolized ev-
erlasting love, on either side of the newlyweds' cottage. If one
or the other took root, this would foretell an imminent wedding for the bridesmaid who planted it.

# ·Not for Unmarried·
# Women Only

For centuries, it was the tradition for bridesmaids to be unmarried women, because supposedly those who had not married represented purity. In this century, brides have placed a high value on friendship and have opted to surround themselves with their most loving friends, married or not.

"Three times a bridesmaid . . . never a bride," is an old saying dating to about the sixteenth century. At wedding feasts in those times, unmarried maidens attended the bride for as many days as the food and drink held out. During these days and nights, bridesmaids were observed assisting the bride in a variety of ways: If the bride was overcome with emotion and required a vial of smelling salts, or a fan to cool her brow, a bridesmaid would help; if the bride needed someone to arrange her wedding dress or robes as she moved about the endless feast, a bridesmaid would be there at her side.

If after serving as a bridesmaid three times the young maiden was unable to catch the eye of unmarried males, then it was thought she never would. However, what many people don't realize is that the rest of that old rhyme quoted above promises that after seven times a bridesmaid, the spell was broken—and a woman was thought to be a sure bet for marriage.

## • *Junior Bridesmaids* •

*W*hat is a junior bridesmaid? It is a charming niche carved into the wedding party just for young girls who are too old to be flower girls, but too young to be bridesmaids. Usually twelve years old and up to mid-teens, junior bridesmaids dress in a style similar to that of the "official" bridesmaids. They look enchanting walking down the aisle in pairs. Usually they precede the flower girls and follow the bridesmaids. Whether or not they stand on the reception line depends on the bride's estimate of their stamina and maturity.

## • *Flower Girls* •

*E*verybody's favorites! The sentimental darlings of the wedding party, flower girls are so captivating that it's nearly impossible for them not to steal the scene from the bride. A wise bride will reflect on this before incorporating too many adorable children into her wedding party!

Children have long been associated with weddings. Procreation was the point of most marriages until this century, and the presence of young children at the celebration underscored this purpose, while imparting an extra measure of good fortune to the bride. Starting with the earliest Greek and Roman weddings, young girls were a significant part of the bridal procession, strewing grains and herbs in the bride's path as symbols of fruitfulness. In medieval times, it was the custom for two young girls, preferably sisters who were dressed identically, to walk before the bride, carrying sheaves of wheat.

Romance bloomed in Elizabethan times along with flowers cultivated in the great gardens of Europe. New varieties were brought back from distant lands only to pop up in the wedding bouquets of the wealthier classes. The young girls of that time who walked before the bride carried nosegays of roses, dianthus, foxglove, and other garden exotica. The flower girl had arrived.

While flower girls are famous for carrying flowers, they also wear them. With a wreath of flowers circling their heads, they continue one of the oldest of wedding traditions. The wreath, an enduring symbol of innocence, has been a part of weddings for over two thousand years.

In Victorian times, flower girls carried precious nosegays of blossoms styled after the bride's bouquet, or ornamental baskets of rose petals. Hoops, wrapped with ribbons and tied with small garlands of flowers, were other turn-of-the-century favorites. Traditionally, flower girls dressed in smaller versions of the bridemaids' outfits, since before the twentieth century, most children were usually clothed in replicas of adult fashion anyway. Present-day flower girls could not be more charming than when they are dressed in gowns or frocks that echo the Victorian era. Pinafores and aprons can be worn in wonderful, simple cottons in the summer, organdy in winter.

Straw hats make pleasing alternatives to garlands for flower girls. Since the hats have a circular shape, they, too, symbolize innocence and eternity. Trim them with lilacs or pansies in the spring, roses in June, asters and bachelor buttons in summer.

## · A *Flock of Flower Girls* ·

*A*s we've seen, there is a long-established precedent for having more than one flower girl. In many European weddings, especially in France and England, it is the custom to have only children attendants. Especially popular with royalty, or near-royalty, this is a charming idea for every type of wedding, whatever the degree of formality.

# · How Old Are Flower Girls? ·

U sually, flower girls should be at least five years old; it's difficult to control children below that age. For this reason, plus the aforementioned scene-stealing potential, it's best to limit the part to children who are old enough to follow instructions.

# · Ring Bearers, Page Boys ·

W hen Queen Elizabeth II (then Princess Elizabeth) married Philip Mountbatten, the duke of Edinburgh, in 1947, despite post–World War II rationing, she was able to wear a wedding gown with a magnificent eighteen-foot train (she was, after all, a crown princess). Accompanying her up the aisle were two page boys wearing Highland kilts and black velvet jackets. Even if you're not a princess, if you do plan to have a highly formal ceremony and wear a gown with a long train, you, too, may need assistance.

The maid of honor customarily takes command of the train, folding it carefully as the bride is seated in her car or carriage. When the train is very long, pages are often included in the wedding party. They hold the train aloft as the bride sweeps up and down the aisle. As this is something that

*All thoughts, all*
*passions, all delights,*
*Whatever stirs this*
*mortal frame,*
*All are but ministers*
*of Love,*
*And feed his sacred*
*flame.*

SAMUEL TAYLOR COLERIDGE:
*"Love"*

❧

requires dexterity and concentration, brides select young boys of a manageable age—about seven to ten is fine. If you'd like pages in your procession, try to select boys who are about the same height for a balanced presentation.

## · To Page or Not to Page ·

S ome people wonder if having pages may be a little excessive. But page boys have been a part of weddings for centuries; some historians trace them back as far as medieval times. In the past, since mostly royal or society weddings were recorded, the tradition of the page has associations of grandeur. Whether or not you use page boys depends upon the degree of formality of your wedding, the length of your train, and your comfort. Please don't feel you have to have page boys because of family pressures (we know your twin nephews are adorable); do it because it makes you feel special.

If you wish to have a ring bearer for sentimental reasons, or because you're having a very formal wedding, carefully consider the job requirements. While the ring bearer has traditionally been a young boy between the ages of three and seven, many regard this as a difficult age to control. Ring bearers carry the bride's ring, or in the case of the double-ring ceremony, both rings, on a ring pillow. This may be tricky; most etiquette experts advise tying the ring or rings to the pillow with a bit of satin ribbon sewn on with a few delicate stitches.

Traditionally, most ring pillows are covered with white satin, frilled with ribbons and lace. A charming wedding present (from a friend or even from yourself) would be a small needlepoint pillow embroidered with the married couple's initials. Or, for a winter wedding, nothing looks richer than velvet in a deep holiday hue.

## · The Groom's Attendants: · Best Man

Screams fill the air, a young maiden struggles as she is scooped up. Not stopping to look back, the groom and groomsman streak off with their bounty. Sound like a lurid romance novel? It's merely what passed for marriage before the days of stretch limousines and bridal registries.

And who was at the groom's side? Then, as now, it was a male friend, a comrade ready to act as needed. It's been many centuries since the days of marriage by capture. But despite its loss, this tradition of male friendship remains intact. After the custom of betrothal became widespread, the role changed to that of a best friend who stood by (now peacefully) to help his comrade during this emotional time of his life.

## · What Makes a Best Man · Great?

*T*he best man is really an advance man, par excellence. The ideal best man has great compassion for his friend, and the best assistance he can give this day is to relieve the groom of anxiety. He knows how to tie a bow tie. He knows where to keep the wedding ring, and he takes great care not to drop it, because he knows the old superstition that it's bad luck to do so. He knows where to stand at the ceremony (to the groom's right). The best man is also one of the two witnesses who sign the bridal registry. And, traditionally, he is the one to give a donation to the official who marries the couple.

Before the ceremony, the best man is briefed as to the seating arrangements: whether anyone requires a special place; where to seat which guests; how to handle latecomers, or those needing any other special assistance. He then quietly lifts this burden from the bride and groom and makes sure that the ushers know how to handle things. And after the ceremony, the best man will drive the newlyweds to the reception, if an automobile has not been hired for this purpose.

## ·The Toast·

Look down you gods
And on this couple drop a blessed crown.

William Shakespeare:
The Tempest

O f all the wonderful things a best man does for his friend, making a heartfelt toast at the reception is probably the most special. Many think that the first toast is traditionally the best man's duty. Certainly, his voice has a place in the festivities; whether he toasts the couple before or after someone else is not what matters. What does matter is that when he speaks, his words be simple and sincere.

Grow old along with me!
The best is yet to be,
The last of life, for which the first was made.
Our times are in his hand.

Robert Browning:
"Rabbi Ben Ezra"

Stirring poems and prose make wonderful substitutes for the best man struggling with a choice of words for the toast. A gift of a book of wedding readings would be a useful and considerate gesture from the groom to his best man.

## • The Ushers •

*L*ong ago, the bride was attended by male friends and family, known as brides' knights. Most recently, the role of the ushers has been to escort guests to their places prior to the wedding service. They may then return to the wedding party and precede the bridesmaids down the aisle. Following the ceremony, ushers may also escort elderly or honored guests from the service.

## • Parents of the Bride • and Groom

"*G*ood mothers are married again at their daughters' weddings," said William Makepeace Thackeray in *Vanity Fair*. The parents of the bride and groom are, of course, an important part of wedding preparations and the celebration itself. At one time, all wedding negotiations took place between them. Today, parents' roles may range from the sole hosts of the wedding, to cohosts with the other set of parents, or simply guests at their children's celebration.

Traditionally, the father of the bride has answered the question, "Who gives this woman away?" because in the past, a daughter was the property of her father. Today, this is strictly optional, although most brides do want to walk down the aisle or stand at the altar with a father or a father figure. If the bride's parents are divorced and she has a stepfather, it is her choice whom she wants to escort her.

In many Jewish ceremonies, the bride will walk to the *huppah*, or to the altar, with both her mother and father. At Christian ceremonies, the mother of the bride is seated last. This is a cue that soon the bridal party will be entering.

In some parts of the country, it's a lovely old tradition for the bride's mother to host a small breakfast on the morning of the wedding for the bridal party. If this interests your mother, you could suggest lots of fresh fruit, light rolls, and if there aren't too many vegetarians present, something sustaining like a Virginia ham.

## • Guests of Honor •

Sometimes, a bride and groom wish to accord special recognition to a guest or guests for whom there is no exact slot in the traditional wedding party. They may be grandparents, godparents, a favorite aunt or uncle, family pastor or doctor, or old friends who are traveling great distances. For them, the designation of *honored guests* is most suitable. While presumably all guests at one's wedding are to be honored, a particular tribute to these loved ones is in order. It's a fine tradition to seat them in a place of importance, acknowledge them in a toast, or dedicate a dance or song to them. Nosegays that match the bridal flowers are a beautiful gesture that say, "You are one of us."

## · Gifts for the Wedding Party ·

So far he [the bridegroom] was reasonably sure of having fulfilled all his obligations. The bridesmaids' eight bouquets of white lilac and lilies-of-the-valley had been sent in due time, as well as the gold and sapphire sleeve-links of the eight ushers and the best man's cat's-eye scarf-pin.

*Edith Wharton:*
THE AGE OF INNOCENCE

One of the most time-honored wedding traditions is that of the bride and groom giving thanks to their wedding party by presenting them with personal gifts. For the maid of honor and bridesmaids, this might take place at a bridesmaids' tea hosted by the bride. Or it could be at the rehearsal dinner, when the groom presents his gifts to the best man and ushers.

In the wildly romantic Elizabethan era, most of the guests were given elaborate gifts from the groom. Traditionally, the bridesmaids and groomsmen were thanked with beautiful silk scarves and precious bits of finery.

White kid leather gloves were the classic gifts for bridesmaids until this century. What other kinds of gifts are customary? Queen Victoria presented each of her bridesmaids with a brooch in the shape of an eagle set with turquoise and pearls. Other Victorian favorites were bracelets, lockets, chokers, handkerchieves, lace scarves, and perfume bottles. In the romantic days of the bride's knights, the bride would give these special men small tokens of her appreciation. Now transformed into present-day ushers, these close friends still receive gifts, often from the groom. Tickets to sporting events, crystal decanters, and fine writing instruments are classics.

If you wish to give your parents a special memento of your appreciation, a silver picture frame or handmade photo album is always appreciated.

*Chapter Six*

# The Bride's Ensemble

## • The Wedding Gown •

HER DRESS WAS A RICH WHITE SATIN, TRIMMED WITH ORANGE FLOWER
BLOSSOMS. ON HER HEAD SHE WORE A WREATH OF THE SAME BLOSSOMS,
OVER WHICH, BUT NOT SO AS TO CONCEAL HER FACE, A BEAUTIFUL VEIL OF
HONITON LACE WAS THROWN. HER BRIDESMAIDS AND TRAIN-BEARERS WERE
SIMILARLY ATTIRED, SAVE THEY HAD NO VEILS.

*The Times,*
FEBRUARY 11, 1840, DESCRIBING THE MARRIAGE OF QUEEN VICTORIA

t is only fitting that any discussion of the wedding gown open on a note of tribute to the one bride responsible for inspiring the wedding dress concept so deeply embedded in our modern psyche. She wasn't a fashionable person, she wasn't even slender, nor was she known for her beauty. She lived for her work, a rare thing for a woman in 1840. She was enormously wealthy and could have afforded any wedding she wanted. Who was this extraordinary woman? None other than Queen Victoria, and what she wore at her wedding changed the way brides dressed for the next one hundred and fifty years.

What was it about her bridal costume that was so remarkable? It started a tradition that is so much a part of the wedding sensibility that most brides think it always existed—the all-white wedding ensemble: white dress, veil, flowers. Certainly, brides married in white before Queen Victoria, but they also married in mauves, soft grays, blues, pastels, browns, reds, and earth tones. There was no dominant wedding color. Victoria's pure-white look changed all that. Her delicate white lace veil gently brushed her fingertips. Her soft, flowing, white satin gown with its deep neckline, full skirt, and flounces of lace endowed her with a loveliness of almost fairy-tale quality. This, coupled with the fact that she was a queen, cast a spell over royal fashion followers, and generations of brides have been dressing like royalty ever since.

Victoria's ensemble was remarkable in other ways. Before her wedding, royal brides were encumbered with heavy robes of velvets and brocades, overly decorated with jewels and embroidery or encased in long gowns of white and silver tissue fabric. Imposing ceremonial jewels added to the burden. Their heads, hardly in the clouds, must have throbbed under the weight of heavy crowns and coronets. When young Princess Charlotte of Brunswick married King George III in 1761 in a gown of white and silver, she was wrapped in such a cumbersome mantle of violet-colored velvet (lined in heavy ermine pelts) that ten attendants were needed to carry it.

Grooms were partly responsible for this uncomfortable state of affairs (the beginning of the honorable tradition of blaming it on the husband!). Up until the eighteenth century, the groom was often the bride's greatest rival for attention. His finery was as magnificent and overdone as hers: satin breeches, brocade vests and overcoats, silk stockings, velvet robes, silver shoe buckles, embroidered lace handkerchiefs. Pity the poor royal bride who had to outshine this splendor.

Prince Albert of Saxe-Coburg-Gotha, Victoria's groom and first cousin, was handsome, tall, slender, and something of a sobersides. He stood to take his vows wearing the relatively somber scarlet-and-white uniform of an officer of the British Guards. His outfit firmly established the newly emerging trend toward more restrained clothes for the groom at the highest levels of the court. This restraint allowed the bride to stand out in contrast, without going to preposterous lengths.

Queen Victoria's gown—and her deceptively simple crown of orange blossoms (twined about the delicate white

*As you are woman, so be lovely.*

ROBERT GRAVES,
*"Pygmalion to Galatea"*

blooms were diamonds from Victoria's vast collection)—
gave brides a model on which to pattern their own weddings.
For here was a twenty-year-old woman who stood at the
head of a great nation. Beauty was the standard by which
women were measured in those days. And though Victoria
was given the highest position by birth, she was denied
beauty. The fact that this young queen had found the great
love of her life—and showed it—touched the hearts of
women, ordinary and aristocratic. Her gown, her garland of
orange blossoms, her white gloves and slippers, all were
poignant and endearing. So evident was Victoria's happiness
that reporters for women's publications were moved to call
this "her hour of beauty."

Overnight, the white, feminine wedding turned into the
new standard. While not every bride could accessorize with
real diamonds and a magnificent diamond-and-sapphire Order of the Garter, the sheer loveliness of Victoria's transfor-
mation was the prize they were inspired to aim for. The only
note of complaint voiced that day was that Victoria's train,
at eighteen feet long, was too short for her bridesmaids to
comfortably arrange themselves around as they escorted the
ecstatic bride up to the altar at the Chapel Royal of St. James
Palace. Other than that, it was Queen Victoria who be-

queathed to every bride since the prerogative to be a beauty on her wedding day.

If Victoria's wedding attire inspired a new bridal tradition, what were brides wearing up to that time? Oddly enough, at the earliest of weddings, the color was white. At ancient Greek celebrations and feast days, young women would dress in flowing robes of white, the color known as their emblem of joy. So it was natural to wear white at something as important as a wedding. At Roman weddings, softly pleated white gowns paid tribute to Hymen, the god of fertility, one of whose favorite colors was white. As a sign of modesty, both Greek and Roman brides covered their heads with flame-colored veils. On their feet they wore sandals of the same vivid intensity:

> Seize the veil of flame-bright hue;
> Joyous come with saffron shoe
> Upon thy foot of snow.
>
> *Gaius Valerius Catullus*

After that, there was no one identifiable tradition in wedding attire; the only note of consistency over the centuries being the garland or crown of flowers. The few bridal styles documented in the past were usually worn by royalty, since their weddings were of historical significance. From 1499, the first record exists of a white royal wedding when Anne of Brittany married Louis XII of France. Four years later, Margaret Tudor, the daughter of England's Henry VII, married wearing a white damask gown edged with crimson, the traditional color of royalty. In another royal marriage, when Princess Elizabeth, daughter of King James I, married in 1612, she wore a dress of silver elaborately embroidered with pearls, silver, and precious stones. This type of dress typifies the royal style that endured until Victoria's wedding.

## · The "One-Time" Dress ·

O nly the very affluent or resourceful could afford the luxury of a dress made solely for the occasion of the wedding, and this condition lasted well into the 1800s. Brides would wear their "Sunday best" dress, or have a dress made of a luxurious and costly material that shifted into their general wardrobes after the ceremony. In 1821, Maria Monroe, daughter of President James Monroe, married in an elegant gown of blue silk embroidered with a motif of red wheat stalks.

Victoria's gown changed this custom, too. Now, the wedding gown was clearly special—a sentimental treasure all the more cherished because of its one-time designated use. The beginning of this tradition coincided with a time when spreading affluence was creating larger middle classes and upper-middle classes that could afford such an indulgence. Oddly enough, there was one occasion when it was socially acceptable to rewear a wedding gown: when being presented at court to none other than Queen Victoria. Her rules governing the dress of ladies were specific and narrow, and the white wedding gown she had inspired fit nicely into those strictures.

Queen Victoria's own daughters married in a style reminiscent of their mother's. Princess Alice married in 1862 wearing a white lace gown puffed up with a newly fashionable crinoline (we are endebted to the crinoline for the extinction of the bustle). Draped around her head and shoulders was a floor-length veil secured by a circle of orange blossoms. Her veil had been designed by her father, whose unexpected death shortly before the wedding cast an unfortunate pall on the affair. Victoria's eldest daughter, Princess Victoria, recalled family tradition at her wedding. Like her mother, her rich white gown was decorated with Honiton lace, and like generations of Windsor

*True love is but a humble, low-born thing, And hath its food served up in earthenware.*

JAMES RUSSELL LOWELL: *"Love"*

brides since, she included orange blossoms and myrtle in her ensemble.

Keeping right in step with the tradition of royal white was the wedding of Empress Eugénie of France to Louis-Napoléon III, in 1853. Renowned for her extraordinary elegance, Eugénie's bridal ensemble exerted further influence on Victorian brides; she wore a dress of velvet and lace, tied back her hair with white hyacinths and lilacs, and carried a simple prayer book.

As America entered the Civil War period, brides married in simple daytime outfits. Once the war ended, however, so too did their restraint, and the bridal gown burst out into the heavily decorated styles so identified with that era. At the turn of the twentieth century, leg-of-mutton sleeves and tiny nipped-in waists created the famous Edwardian silhouette.

War always has an affect on fashion: Following World War I, wedding dresses reflected the social change brewing across the classes. Long-waisted, slim-hipped gowns of satins and silks deemphasized the female body as women broke free in the heyday of the flapper. The severity of the Great Depression let the air out of this balloon pretty quickly, however. Hard times inspire escape through fantasy, and Hollywood was quick to provide movies whose influence seared itself into the national consciousness as brides imitated screen stars in their long, flouncy "tea dresses" and large, garden-party hats.

World War II austerity sent most brides back to marrying in clothes they could wear again. Practical suits of sturdy cloth were popular, as well as heirloom wedding dresses handed down from family members. In 1951, Margaret Thatcher, the future prime minister of Great Britain, wore a blue velvet dress for her wedding, which apparently became a favorite part of her wardrobe.

But the vision of loveliness forever etched into the bridal consciousness of the all-white "Cinderella" wedding could not be kept down. It reappeared with a vengeance in the 1950s and 1960s as hairstyles grew higher, tiaras more ornate, gowns fuller and more elaborate. Elizabeth Taylor's 1950 wedding defined the beginning of this era when she married in the quintessential "fairy-tale" gown of white satin with a tight princess waistline and full flowing skirt. It was a rare case of life triumphant over art—she actually looked more lovely than she did in the 1954 movie *Father of the Bride.*

Today, brides are in the best fashion position they've ever enjoyed. With the panorama of history spread before and behind them, they may follow in the great tradition of the all-white wedding inspired by Victoria; or they may dress in brightly hued velvets like a Renaissance princess, or enrobe themselves in simple, delicate shifts of linen and lace. A bride can slip a beautiful lace apron over her dress as did Colonial brides, or she may choose an ethnic garment that reflects her heritage: an Indian sari, a Japanese kimono.

Queen Victoria's ensemble set brides on a new path. It gave them the right to be anything they wanted to be. While there will always be brides who want to be practical and plan a wedding outfit that will be worn again, most brides today cherish their wedding gowns as "once-in-a-lifetime" treasures to enhance their weddings, say something about themselves, and then afterward, be preserved in leaves of tissue—perhaps for their own daughters or granddaughters.

## · Colors ·

MARRIED IN WHITE, YOU HAVE CHOSEN ALL RIGHT,
MARRIED IN GRAY, YOU WILL GO FAR AWAY,
MARRIED IN BLACK, YOU WILL WISH YOURSELF BACK,
MARRIED IN RED, YOU WILL WISH YOURSELF DEAD,
MARRIED IN GREEN, ASHAMED TO BE SEEN,
MARRIED IN BLUE, HE WILL ALWAYS BE TRUE,
MARRIED IN PEARL, YOU WILL LIVE IN A WHIRL,
MARRIED IN YELLOW, ASHAMED OF YOUR FELLOW,
MARRIED IN BROWN, YOU WILL LIVE OUT OF TOWN,
MARRIED IN PINK, YOUR SPIRIT WILL SINK.

*Old English rhyme*

*A*ccording to this popular rhyme, there are very few colors a sane bride would think of wearing. Color, at a wedding, has a lore all its own, with as many superstitions attendant to it as there are hues in the rainbow. Putting the pervasive all-white wedding aside for a moment, we can see a wealth of other bridal traditions before us.

According to the old rhyme above, a bride had to have been fairly selective about the color of her wedding gown. Prior to the mid-1800s, all the colors mentioned in the rhyme appeared as frequently at weddings as they did in daily life. White was the most luxurious color choice quoted because, except in the summer, there wasn't much call for white. It was still the color of innocence, and no bride could go wrong with it. Gray was seen in many "traveling outfits," or more formal suits used for visiting, shopping, or church. Black, the color associated with heavy mourning, was worn when circumstances demanded it. Observing the proper etiquette of mourning was essential, making little or no concessions to weddings. This rhyme may not have been translated into Spanish, however, because in Spain, it is an old-fashioned tradition for Roman Catholic brides to wear fancy, lacy, black gowns. After the wedding, the gowns are then dedicated to an image of the Virgin Mary.

Brides wearing red might "wish themselves dead," because

red was thought to proclaim a person of easy virtue. This is not true in the eastern part of the world, though. To the Chinese and Hindus, this color of power promises good tidings, and so it is especially welcome at weddings. Early-American brides made wearing red a patriotic gesture during the Revolutionary War, as red, the symbol of the colonies, blazed brightly at many weddings in support of the valiant cause of independence. On another patriotic note, during the Civil War, many brides selected purple wedding dresses to honor the war dead. Purple is the color of virtue and valor, as exemplified by the award of the Purple Heart.

And "something blue": If you're thinking of a very spiritual color other than white for your gown, blue is the choice that embodies the historical as well as the spiritual. Blue is the ancient color of purity, love, and fidelity, and it possesses many religious associations. Ancient Hebrew brides married in white gowns trimmed with bands of blue. This color of the heavens is also the color ascribed to the robe of the Virgin Mary. Those named Mary are said to have a special affinity for blue, and it's an old tradition for them to marry wearing a bit of this color. We know of one monarch who did. At her first wedding, Mary, Queen

*And this maiden she lived with no other thought Than to love and be loved by me.*

EDGAR ALLAN POE:

*"Annabel Lee"*

of Scots, was enrobed in a spectacular dark blue velvet gown heavily decorated with jewels and white embroidery. On her head she wore a glorious gold coronet of jewels. One of the most famous brides of the twentieth century, Wallis Simpson, wore a pale blue gown designed by Mainbocher for her 1937 marriage to a man who had once been king—the duke of Windsor.

Yellow is rarely seen as a bridal color—even in remarriages or weddings of older brides. Despite its being another hue associated with the Greek god of marriage and fertility, Hymen, so many believed that yellow promotes that white-hot passion, jealousy, that it has been avoided for centuries. Even yellow flowers seem to share this stigma and are a rare sight at weddings. "Yellow by the saints forsworn" has been an amber caution light to brides for years, one which they apparently heed.

But nearly everyone agrees that green is *the* worst wedding color of all. "Nothing green for a fine day," brides are warned in another rhyme. Green isn't a "bad" color, but for one thing, it's very hard to wear; even Kermit the Frog laments, "it's not easy being green." While some poets find rejuvenation and promise in this color of nature, it has traditionally been avoided by brides—except the Norwegian bride, who sees it differently. In her country, green is a treasured color, long a part of bridal wardrobe.

One deviation from the Victorian obsession with the all-white wedding occurred late in the 1800s. Many American and European brides flocked to wear colors created from new aniline, or synthetic, dyes. Sharp browns, russets, crimson, blues, and yarrow soon appeared in stores. The Victorians, eager to embrace any new development, took up these colors, and the fashionable worked them into their wedding wardrobes.

White and all its variations—ivory, ecru, champagne, cream—are wonderful at any wedding, though it's been a tradition in the past not to wear these tones for remarriage, or if the bride is of older years. What did the bride wear if not white? Soft pastels, grays, delicate shades. Fortunately, this restriction is disappearing with other tradition-bound ways. Women are more career-oriented, are marrying later in life, and so, too, is remarriage an accepted part of our culture. We are starting to realize that on their wedding day, all brides are equal and are entitled to wear whatever makes them happy.

## · V e i l s ·

*H*er wedding is probably the only time in a woman's life when she will wear a veil, except perhaps for the long black veil associated with funerals. But the wedding is a joyful affair and it seems right for the bride to want to feel the light-as-air softness of a veil caressing her face and shoulders.

A tradition from earliest Greek and Roman civilizations right up to today, the veil has had a wildly romantic past and has meant different things at different times. But one belief common to Christian, Jewish, Moslem, and Hindu religions alike is that the wedding veil is a symbol of purity. To some, the veil protected the bride, who was susceptible to the stares of jealous or "evil spirits" believed to be ever-present, particularly at times of happiness.

The bright scarlet or flame-colored veils of the Greeks betokened modesty and homage before their god of marriage, Hymen. After the ceremony, Grecian brides made an offering of their veils to Hera, deity of marriage and protector of women, as a way of helping ensure successful childbirth. The Vestal Virgins wore veils as a symbol of devotion to the gods. But some have attributed a more sinister origin to the veil: that it traces to women being wrapped up in cloths by grooms on horseback in the earliest days of brides by capture. In order to fool marauding would-be grooms, women kept covered in veils—and sometimes the "brides" who were captured were a surprise—older women from the tribe who were well past childbearing age.

## · Lifting the Veil ·

Some believe the veil tradition originated in the days when bridal parties set out on foot or horseback to the wedding. Traveling together, the bridal caravan advanced under a large canopy. This custom showed up in a streamlined version at Anglo-Saxon weddings as men sheltered the bride under a cloth. This cloth or "veil" was thought to symbolize the bride's status as part of her father's house, under his control. When the ceremony was completed, the veil was lifted and the bride emerged, no longer her parents' property, but a married woman. This is the genesis of two traditions: the bride walking to the altar with her face covered, and lifting her veil after taking her vows.

Gradually, the veil became a part of the bridal ensemble itself, either attached to the bride's wreath or coronet, or draped simply over her shoulders.

The popularity of veils waxed and waned but never completely disappeared. Victoria's wedding clearly reestablished them. One of the reasons for their scarcity was their expense. Veils were handmade of beautiful lace, costing great sums. Queen Victoria's veil of Honiton lace made in Devon (which, prophetically, she had ordered well before her engagement) was said to have cost over a thousand pounds. This was an astronomical sum in the days when women like Elizabeth Barrett Browning's loyal maid Wilson were paid sixteen pounds a year. Many veils were so valuable that the same one was handed down from generation to generation, giving rise to the notion that it was good luck to borrow one. Thus, the veil became the "something borrowed" in the famous rhyme. A veil that had sheltered happily married women was especially prized. Sometimes, after the wedding, Victorian ladies would press their veils into service as shawls, or as coverings at balls.

American wedding lore has its own bridal-veil story, dating back to early Colonial days when a young woman named Nellie Custis married an aide of President George Washington. She is credited with beginning the veil tradition in our new nation. According to the story, Nellie was seated next to a window with her face shrouded by a pretty lace curtain. Her husband-to-be walked by, and the vision of loveliness he glimpsed made him fall instantly in love. In memory of

*What woman, however old, has not the bridal favours and raiment stowed away, and packed in lavender, in the inmost cupboards of her heart.*

WILLIAM MAKEPEACE
THACKERAY

this romantic moment, Nellie, who was apparently clever as well as beautiful, wore a lace veil at her wedding.

Lace often substituted for costly veils, even though lace itself was expensive. More of an accent than a theme, it was especially pretty on bonnets. Many a bride in the 1700s and early 1800s would take her Sunday-best bonnet and decorate it with a row of lace peeking out from under the brim. But lace was still handmade, and it was not until the availability of machine-made lace that lavishly trimmed veils were seen at greater numbers of weddings.

When that happened, wedding dresses were bedecked with as much lace as the overly ornamented "wedding cake" architecture of the period. Where lace was once a trim, it now engulfed the entire gown. Yards and yards of the frothy white stuff was flounced, tucked, and pinned to make gowns. Upswept hairstyles were fastened with lace, handkerchiefs were bordered with it, even wedding parasols received an icing of this fanciful trim.

Lace remains a cherished part of the bridal ensemble. Many brides wear family heirloom veils. Others have beautiful lace pieces comissioned for them. Grace Kelly wore a gown sewn with three hundred and twenty yards of Valenciennes lace in her 1956 marriage to Prince Rainier of Monaco. In 1953, when Jacqueline Bouvier married Senator John

F. Kennedy, her stunning floor-length veil was held to her head by a modest maiden's cap of lace. More recent royal brides, Princess Diana, and our own American royalty, Caroline Kennedy, have dressed in luscious sweeps of lace embroidered with symbols that have personal meaning for them.

An old bride's superstition tells us that it's bad luck to try on a veil before a wedding—or to let another woman try it on. She might try to steal your fiancé!

## · T r a i n s ·

Queen Victoria's seminal wedding gown with its eighteen foot train of white satin and lace spun off another regal flourish—the bridal train. Brides are sometimes confused about what a train actually is: Is it a long veil, is it something separate that attaches to the shoulders of the wedding gown, or does it flow from the skirt?

The longest and most formal version is the cathedral train, spilling anywhere from nine to eighteen feet behind the bride. The shortest is the sweep train usually just brushing the floor for a foot or two. A chapel train is a full-shaped skirt made from yards and yards of fabric with a foot or less of train trailing behind. Some trains are detachable and can be removed before the reception.

What is the purpose of a train? They've always been a part of royal garb, the length of the train corresponding to the importance of the occasion and the position of the wearer. When brides decided to pattern themselves after royalty, the "court train" entered into the bridal tapestry. Worth of Paris, the most influential clothing designer of the Victorian era, designed wedding dresses with a variety of trains for his society clients, but the best-loved one was the very long train. Trains may be anything from simple net tulle to expensive fabrics trimmed with lace, pearls, or orange blossoms. Since brides so prominently hold the spotlight on their wedding day, there is no such thing as excess, and they may wear a gown with any length train that pleases them.

Flowing from a modest three feet to twenty-five feet, as seen on Princess Diana's satin gown, long trains require the assistance of bridal attendants. First the train must be arranged in a graceful sweep before the bride walks down the aisle. It's long been part of the bridal attendants' duties to help carry the train to protect it from damage. This is done by bridesmaids, such as in Victoria's wedding, or page boys. Some brides, such as Diana's mother-in-law, Queen Elizabeth II, love the look of young page boys in kilts of royal tartans and velvet jackets. Two well-behaved lads carried the eighteen foot ivory silk tulle train she wore at her wedding in 1947.

Other brides love to let the train spill forth by itself, an especially pretty sight on a dark-carpeted church aisle.

## · *Tiaras* ·

*T*iaras reinforce the image that the bride is a queen, or at least a princess. An etiquette expert from the early 1900s advised young brides that the tiara was appropriate to wear on one's wedding day, but not before, as one would be assumed to be mature enough to carry it off only when ready for marriage. Certainly, real royalty had been doing this for centuries, and what was good enough for them was good enough for the average bride. The tiara turned out to be a major wedding icon that rivals the simple garland or wreath of flowers.

Tiaras made from real gemstones—usually diamonds— are most likely to be museum-quality collectibles belonging to only a few women in the world besides royalty. Americans have little history of wearing tiaras at occasions other than weddings, their regal associations being inappropriate. Most of the tiaras crowning brides today are of the frankly fake variety, but that doesn't dim their sparkle or the gleam in the bride's eye.

## •Headdresses•

*P*ractically every bride marries wearing some type of ornamentation on her head. History tells us that the wreath or garland of flowers was the earliest form of headdress, lasting right through the Middle Ages, Renaissance, Elizabethan and Victorian eras to our time.

Apart from garlands or wreaths, headdresses can be anything from a beautiful antique ivory-and-silver comb holding back an upswept hairstyle studded with baby's breath, to bunches of gilded myrtle leaves glistening with pearls. Combining the glamour of jewelry with the loveliness of flowers, headdresses can be worn alone or attached to a veil. They might be bonnets with lace and flowers, even riding hats, with delicate white veils draped over the eyes.

Practically all cultures wear some form of headdress. For example, Swedish brides wear elaborate crowns, while Greek brides wear narrow white bands tied with white satin ribbons.

## • *Accessories* •

> Mama came before me and brought me a nosegay
> of orange flowers. . . . I wore a white satin gown with
> a very deep flounce of Honiton lace, imitation of
> old. I wore my Turkish diamond necklace and
> earrings, and Albert's beautiful sapphire brooch.
>
> *Queen Victoria:*
> JOURNAL, February 10, 1840

*A* bridal gown is so outside the norm of everyday beauty that it has traditionally required accessorizing of an equally magnificent character. Few brides stop with just a wonderful dress—they go on to add earrings, necklace, gloves, and purse to heighten the image presented. While not every bride possesses a "beautiful sapphire brooch" (Victoria was following the English custom of pinning a brooch over the heart to symbolize wedding day innocence), brides do dress up with family heirlooms and their own best pieces.

The pearl strand, a beloved modern-day wedding fixture, is a tradition of fairly recent vintage. Our ancestors avoided pearls because they were thought to resemble real tears. Also, during the days when "free-range" pearls were harvested by hand, they were beyond the reach of most brides. Seed pearls are different; being machine-made and inexpensive, galaxies of them have added their sheen to gowns for the past century or so.

Courting couples have always given each other gifts of jewelry. But in the very socially regulated Victorian era, gifts had to substitute for more earthly expressions of love. Bridegrooms were permitted to give gold lockets, necklaces, watches, fans, or earrings, and it was a tradition to wear a particularly treasured gift from the groom on the wedding day. Victorian brides were instructed that if their wedding took place in the morning, the bride could wear only jewelry given to her by the groom. We don't know what the consequences would have been otherwise!

White gloves, formerly an indispensable part of every proper young lady's wardrobe, have all but disappeared from the bridal repertoire along with fans and smelling salts. It's really a loss, because long white kid gloves or lacy hand-crocheted mittens add an elegant exclamation point to a dazzling wedding statement. Edwardian brides embroidered their gloves with wedding symbols, and often beautiful examples of these survive in vintage clothing shops. Certainly our great-grandmothers would not have married without them, even though an old English superstition tells us that a maiden does not wear gloves for her wedding—only a widow remarrying!

If you choose to marry wearing gloves, remember, you may pass them, along with your bouquet, over to your maid of honor just before exchanging rings.

The Bride's Ensemble

# ·The Handkerchief and Favours·

LIKE STREAMERS IN THE PAINTED SKY,

AT EVERY BREAST THE FAVOURS FLY.

*Edward Chicken:*
"THE COLLIER'S WEDDING"

*I*n the Elizabethan era, both men and women decorated their bridal finery with gaily colored ribbons called favours. The ribbons were predominately silver or gold if the wedding was royal, or white and blue ("something blue") for everyone else. They signified the fastness of the wedding union, and dated all the way back to earliest northern civilizations when marrying entailed, literally, "tying the knot"—primitive men and women being bound together with ropes around their waists. Now, in the sixteenth century, brides were tying love knots and favours all over their gowns.

Somewhere in their sleeve or bodice, brides made room for a delicate handkerchief. Embroidered with the bride and groom's name or monogram, these were very beautiful and very practical, considering how emotional a wedding is. What a lovely tradition to revive. Certainly, an antique lace or silk handkerchief, pressed and framed, would be a special memento to hang in a new home after the wedding. Don't wash out the tear stains—they'll add to its allure.

## · Garters ·

W hat's a wedding without a garter? Garters, in the age of panty hose, are exclusively ceremonial, not functional. Usually made of a luxurious material such as satin trimmed with lace, the garter was always worn by the bride from Elizabethan through Victorian days. At early bedding ceremonies following the wedding feast, the bride and groom were escorted into the bridal chamber amid much raucous fun with their groomsmen and bridesmaids. As part of the celebration, the groom's friends attempted to snatch garters from the bride. Predictably, some brides didn't like this practice and threw their own garters at the assembled crowd before being mauled. Thus began the tradition of throwing the garter. Nowadays, this usually takes place at the reception, if at all, and often, the garter becomes the "something blue" every bride needs.

## · Shoes ·

F or centuries, shoes have been a symbol of authority and possession. Among early civilizations shoes were exchanged to seal a bargain. This evolved into a father of the bride giving his daughter shoes as part of her dowry, or to the groom to signify handing over control. In Greece, the groom gives the bride a new pair of shoes, and in Bulgaria, the bride receives "shoe money." Even Cinderella had to fit into the right shoe before she found her true prince and happiness.

It's also an old superstition that evil spirits fear leather. The bridegroom would leave a shoe outside the bridal chamber door on the wedding night. And when we see old shoes tied to the back of newlyweds' cars, or thrown at them after the reception, this is what this frivolity signifies. In the Orient, a red shoe thrown on the top of a roof is a signal that honeymooners are inside.

Until this century, most brides wore sweet bridal slippers or low heeled shoes with their bridal gowns. These slippers of satin and silk were extraordinarily beautiful, hand-embroidered or trimmed with lace and flowers. Some survive in museum costume collections and are marvels of daintiness and loveliness.

*Chapter Seven*

# The Bride's Trousseau

DON'T FORGET THE KITCHEN WHEN YOU ARE PURCHASING YOUR HOUSEHOLD
LINENS. THIS IS THE BUSINESS END OF THE HOUSEHOLD AND NEEDS TO BE
AS WELL EQUIPPED AS ANY OTHER ROOM. AGAIN, QUALITY IS IMPORTANT,
FOR IF THE TOWELS ARE NOT PROPERLY ABSORBENT, THE CHINA WILL NOT
DRY EASILY AND SILVER AND GLASSES WILL BE STREAKED. ALSO THE
BETTER-QUALITY TOWELS WILL NOT LEAVE LINT ON ANY ARTICLES WIPED. IN
THE LINEN DEPARTMENTS OF THE LARGER DEPARTMENT STORES YOU WILL
FIND TOWELS WITH THE WORDS "GLASS TOWEL" OR "KITCHEN TOWEL"
WOVEN IN THE MATERIAL. BUY SEVERAL OF EACH IF YOUR BUDGET ALLOWS
FOR IT.

> *Marguerite Bentley:*
> WEDDING ETIQUETTE COMPLETE

The above passage from an etiquette book published at the start of the post–World War II
"baby boom" is fascinating. It's from a section

entitled "Your Linen Trousseau," and in addition to its undeniable quaintness, it attests to the social changes that have taken place since its writing. While our mothers may have been advised to stock up on two different types of dish towels, it's a rare bride today who has the time to dry the dishes—or the space in which to store an array of kitchen linens. Besides, the dishwasher has taken over the drying, and other kitchen chores are now often democratically shared by husband and wife. As for dining with china, silver, and crystal, unfortunately, for most of us today, these luxuries are "company-only" treats.

Nonetheless, the trousseau is one of the most time-honored of all wedding traditions dating back to earliest recorded history. Most brides are still excited about dressing up their new homes, and the urge to build a nest is a compelling instinct. There is something so comforting and cozy about the idea of a trousseau, perhaps because it affirms the importance of the home, that it is to be hoped that this gentle custom never completely disappears from the bridal scene.

But the trousseau tradition has changed dramatically, especially in this century—so much so that many brides wonder: Exactly what is a trousseau? Is it fancy lingerie? Is it the clothes a bride takes on her honeymoon, or beautiful personal toiletry items for her dressing table? The trousseau can be all that—and more.

The most traditional trousseau was once a collection of all the possessions a young woman would carefully assemble to take with her into her marriage, including useful household objects and family keepsakes of great sentimental value. The word *trousseau* itself has a charming origin, deriving from the French *trusse*, meaning little bundle. Images come to mind of the bride, like a brave adventurer, entering her new world with a little bundle of her handmade possessions tied up in cloth.

The typical eighteenth- and nineteenth-century trousseau was large, encompassing linens, lingerie, clothing, and all the bride's finery. Comfort and warmth in the bedrooms (master, children's, guests') was essential, so the bride-to-be collected pillows, blankets, quilts, coverlets, and linens, hand-embroidered if time permitted. The kitchen was next in importance. Utensils had to last a lifetime, so brides wanted high-quality tools for the hearth, plus brooms, tablecloths, fine china, silver, and crystal. The bathroom didn't really exist as such until late in the 1800s, but there were hip baths and washbowls requiring plenty of towels, cloths, and other necessities.

It was for her own welfare that the bride gathered her

*Never change when love has found its home.*

SEXTUS PROPERTIUS:
*Elegies*

greatest harvest, putting together an ample supply of clothes and undergarments: pretty petticoats, chemises, drawers, stockings, nightgowns, dressing robes, day outfits, bonnets, gloves, handbags, shoes, traveling outfits, ball gowns, and more. Three or four afternoon dresses, two summer suits, two tea gowns, two dozen pairs of stockings were considered a start. The farsighted bride put aside enough things to see her through many years' use, because she knew her father's obligation to her ceased once her husband's began. In Victorian days, "a dozen of everything" was considered the bare minimum, and a decent trousseau wardrobe was expected to last at least ten years!

If we look far back in time, we must acknowledge the historical reality that women were viewed in terms of their "marketability." Brides were exchanged in matrimony for currency or something else of value. If part of the package she had to offer included an extensive trousseau, the bride enhanced her chances of marrying well. This attitude softened in time as love entered the mix and young ladies could happily prepare for their futures with someone they adored.

In practically all civilizations, girls realistically prepared for marriage while still very young. Grecian brides stockpiled household goods and clothes. In the sixth and seventh centuries, peasant girls entered marriage with a trousseau of practical housekeeping utensils: homemade baskets, brooms, soaps, bedding, cloth. The brides of the aristocracy could afford trousseaux that included the basics topped off with more luxurious items. They spent their childhoods embroidering clothes and fine underthings. Heavy, hand-carved wooden wardrobes or armoires held robes, tapestries, silver drinking vessels, costly household furnishings, even jewels, as the bride waited for her marriage. But, whatever her means, nearly every bride put together a trousseau, and the tradition continued unchanged until the nineteenth century.

The act of creating a trousseau was both a hobby and a hope—and a tradition passed down from mother to daughter. A mother who cared about her daughter's future would increase that daughter's chances of being treated well in marriage by devoting great energy to making her trousseau impressive in size and scope. Even today, there are vestiges of this in our collective wedding psyche. A famous example is the way Michael Corleone, in Mario Puzo's epic saga of Italian-American life, *The Godfather*, makes sure his brother Sonny's daughter is well provided for as she plans her engagement to the son of a patrician American family.

*I have a chair for you in the smallest parlor in the world, to wit, my heart.*

EMILY DICKINSON

## · The Hope Chest ·

The hope chest is an old tradition born in rural communities in many parts of the world. Thrift and hard work were the values ennobled in our own American pioneer society. Laying aside a supply of household linens was one way mothers prepared their daughters for the future. Many productive hours would be spent weaving fabrics, stitching quilts, sewing, and embroidering linens to grace new homes. Young girls learned the art of needlecraft at a very early age. Winter afternoons and summer evenings would pass peacefully as they stitched their initials onto fine cottons, hemmed cloths for the bath, sewed quilts and counterpanes. When finished, their work would be admired, then carefully folded and placed into a chest or a trunk just for this use. These came to be known as hope chests.

As these chests filled with beautiful things, so, too, did mothers' hearts fill with hopes for their daughters' happiness. The hope chest became both a revered icon and a well-loved piece of furniture safeguarding the daughter's future. Handmade of wood, many were painted or hand-carved with wedding motifs, the daughter's name, and date of birth. As beautiful keepsakes of a bygone era, hope chests are prized

family heirlooms. Others are eagerly sought-after folk treasures in antique shops and auctions.

In the 1800s, immigrants flocking to America brought
their wedding traditions with them. Young Italian girls followed in the footsteps of their mothers and grandmothers,
hand sewing puffy quilts of feathers or down that had been
carefully packed in their shipboard trunks.

By the mid-1800s, most brides had hope chests brimming
with pretty handmade things. But on the horizon loomed a
development that was to have far-ranging consequences for
the traditional trousseau: the Industrial Revolution. Factories
produced goods at an astonishing rate and less expensively
than if handmade. It was no longer necessary to devote a
childhood to sewing items for the home or handcrafting
utensils.

The consumer needed a place to buy these goods. Soon,
the Victorian bride was dazzled by large department stores
springing up in big cities: A. T. Stewart's in New York, John
Wanamaker's in Philadelphia, Filene's of Boston, Marshall
Field's in Chicago. These became her "sewing room" as she
ordered yards and yards of sheeting and terry cloth to be run
up on her new electric sewing machine—or she purchased
her linens ready-made. Aisle after aisle held the promise of
a glowing future with every type of ware for the home. Lin-

*Whoso loves, believes
the impossible:*

ELIZABETH BARRETT
BROWNING:
*"Aurora Leigh"*

gerie departments offered all a bride could desire or use. Dresses, suits, and gowns could be bought in standardized sizes to fit everyone. For those not living near one of these thrilling emporiums, mail order companies such as Sears, Roebuck and Company and Montgomery Ward illustrated page after page of tantalizing trousseau items.

This was the turning point for the trousseau. Because of the newfound ease of obtaining a household object, the focus of the trousseau gradually shifted to personal wardrobes for the bride. The Victorian era bride-to-be was more than happy to devote herself to this task—and the trousseau became a showcase for her personal taste. But old traditions die hard. In 1905, the bride's parents were cautioned by etiquette writers that they were still responsible for providing household linens, sheets, pillows, bedspreads, tablecloths, and napkins. Four dozen towels were a bare necessity!

## • The Trousseau Tea •

A charming Victorian social custom grew out of this heightened interest in the bride's wardrobe trousseau: the trousseau tea. At that time, when most brides held their daytime receptions or wedding breakfasts at home, those who were most fashionable displayed their wedding gifts, perhaps in a study or music room. Lace-covered tables held handsome clocks and lamps, delicate teapots, silver serving pieces by the dozen, and crystal by the caseload. This custom was popular for a while, but soon was criticized for being too showy. So the bride, still wishing to exhibit all her wonderful, expensive wedding presents, hit upon the idea of inviting a few friends over for a trousseau tea party. There, amid bracing cups of Assam tea and trays of petits fours and meringues, the bride not only exhibited her gifts, but was coaxed to show off selections from her newly acquired wardrobe. This is still a sweet way to entertain friends informally before the wedding, and a variation on the bride's traditional tea for the brides-maids. If you're thinking of doing this, be sure your guests do not confuse this gathering with a shower and feel obli-gated to bring presents.

In Emily Post's 1922 book, *Etiquette*, she mused on the great changes that had taken place in the trousseau during that era. Commenting on the trend toward overembellish-ment, she lamented that the trousseau had come to mean expensive clothes for the bride, rather than practical linens for the home. Six decades later, her book was updated and recommended supplying extra hand towels and washcloths for the household's part-time help. In her 1988 *Etiquette: A Guide to Modern Manners*, Charlotte Ford didn't waste anybody's time with advice for the trousseau collector, realistically devoting but a paragraph to discussing monograms for unusual silver pieces.

Today, few people think of the bride's parents as having the obligation to assemble a trousseau, although it is a lovely gesture for a bride to be given a hope chest upon announcing her engagement. This charming piece of furniture can be very useful not only for storing linens and blankets, but as a toy chest—and, hopefully, as a family keepsake to pass along to future generations.

*Love sought is good, but given unsought is better.*

WILLIAM SHAKESPEARE:
*Twelfth Night*

Still, it is hard for the modern bride to abandon the trousseau altogether. Our lifestyles have brought great changes to housekeeping. Many couples live together before marriage, and for others, remarriage eliminates most of the need for a household trousseau. But if the trousseau has now come to mean beautiful things for the bride to wear and to decorate her dressing table, let her indulge herself. It's time for gold hairpins, elegant brush and comb sets, crystal perfume flacons, delicate lingerie and handsome clothes—even those sumptuous lace-edged sheets. In the most time-honored tradition of the trousseau, may every bride gather all these lovely things—her *trusse*—before starting on an exciting journey into a new life.

*Chapter Eight*

# Wedding Day Dressing

To love one maiden only, cleave to her,
And worship her by years of noble deeds.

*Alfred, Lord Tennyson:*
Idylls of the King

he great day dawns, and it's a safe bet that not too many members of the bridal party are well rested—especially if the night before featured a rousing rehearsal dinner or, more draining yet, a bachelor party. No need for coffee today; soon the excited couple's adrenaline levels will soar as they get caught up in the fine old tradition of dressing for the wedding.

A part of nearly every culture, preparation to appear in public as bride and groom involves exciting rituals. For the groom, this has come to mean assistance with his cravat or bow tie; for the bride, a richer scene unfolds in a happy flurry of women-only activity. Tissue paper flies in the air as dresses and lingerie are unfurled. Combs, brushes, cosmetics—all the weaponry for beauty—come to the fore. Bridesmaids reach out to fasten gowns and pin on veils as photographers capture every teardrop and embrace. Thus a late-twentieth-century wedding rite is begun.

But where did this merry tradition come from? Some wedding historians credit it with a gruesome origin, tracing it from ancient days of yore when young women were wrapped in cloths by fellow tribeswomen to prevent kidnapping by men on horseback. As mentioned earlier, some think it was the so-called groom who wrapped the bride, and that later dressing ceremonies were reenactments of that ritual. On the male side, the groom required assistance of the groomsmen to strap on his shields, tunics, and armor. Others think the dressing of the bride and groom developed into an important ritual because it was always necessary to appease household gods during time of change, and being clean or "pure" was a sign of respect. Uncertainty may shroud this tradition, but what we do know is that in the past, both grooms and brides dressed with care.

# ·*The Groom's Raiment*·

No one accustomed to mix with the higher classes
of Society will at all be inclined to dispute the
advantages arising from a genteel appearance; it
therefore becomes necessary that the means of
acquiring this distinction should be clearly
demonstrated.

*H. Le Blanc:*
"THE ART OF TYING THE CRAVAT"

*T*here has long been a tradition of dressing and decorating oneself to "rise to the occasion." Let us not
be fooled into thinking that this applies solely to women.
All too often, it appears that the groom of recent decades is
a guest at his own wedding, viewing the hustle and bustle
with a bemused and tolerant eye—that, indeed, his only duty
has come down to just "showing up." But history won't let
the groom off that easily. All through the recorded past, men,
too, have been preoccupied with fashion and body adornment. Somewhat less concerned than women with the aesthetic appeal of their dress, they are involved with fashion's
message of status, power, and income. As one would expect,
this is especially true at public occasions such as weddings.
Though today the lion's share of attention may go to the

bride, as we look back through history, we can discern an equally glorious figure at her side. For centuries, the groom was grandly enrobed in silks, satins, velvets, and brocades every bit as sumptuous as the bride's.

If you had been a guest at a Greek wedding two thousand years ago, you would have glimpsed the groom dressed in a flowing white toga, an outfit very similar to the bride's. Crowning his head would have been the traditional garland of wheat ears or herbs. But, if it had been the wedding of a patrician, the groom's toga would have been distinguished by borders of crimson, or perhaps a gold tunic glittering atop his toga.

Over the next few centuries, as men and women married, they kept apace in style. For common working folk, usually it was a matter of putting on their best clothes and perhaps festooning themselves with ribbons and flowers. For the prosperous, there were always embellishments. In the eighth century, the groom added a note of luxury with an embroidered or bejeweled vest or tunic. The twelfth century saw the opening of new trade routes and flourishing trade markets. This made possible a more impressive display of wealth as the groom bedecked himself in luxurious velvets, silks, brocades, furs—and jewelry of gemstones, gold, and silver. Both lords and ladies spared no expense on their weddings. They

*'Tis sweet to know there is an eye will mark*
*Our coming and will look better when we come.*

Lord Byron:
*Don Juan*

adorned themselves ostentatiously right throught the eighteenth century, with brief spells of sanity in the court of King James I, whose influence produced a more restrained way of dressing.

If European grooms were fussing with wigs and waistcoats, what was happening in America, home of the rough-hewn frontiersman and the gentrified landowner? The continental influence was felt, but at a safe distance: grooms' dress was simpler, less elaborate. Nevertheless, grooms wore dress suits with stockings and luxurious waistcoats. Some elected to marry wearing the uniforms of the militia, looking dashing in their shiny brasses and sabers.

Still, it was the Victorians who endowed men's fashion with the elegance it possesses today. Operating under strict codes of etiquette, they had an appropriate outfit for every wedding: white tie and tails for ultraformal weddings; a three-piece suit with a frock coat for at-home events. A top hat or bowler, walking stick, gloves, and cravats were notable elegant accessories. Spats, then as now, were optional.

Today's groom is, from a sartorial standpoint, more fortunate than he has ever been. He has much more freedom—but with this has come confusion, and to some, there seem to be too many options. Let loose in the local "Rent-a-Tux" shop, many have no idea of what is appropriate. If your groom wants to be more involved in the planning of the wedding, have a quiet dinner with him and discuss the basics of how you see the wedding shaping up. There is one simple guideline here: The bride's gown sets the degree of formality; from her outfit, all others follow. If you have discovered a gorgeous satin gown with a long train, the groom should match your formality by wearing a cutaway. If you want to marry barefoot on a mountaintop, a soft white shirt and waistcoat would be handsome for him. While the etiquette rules for men's attire have loosened over the past years, always remember: You are marrying the man you love, and if his dream is to look like Fred Astaire, let him wear that top hat, white tie, and tails; you would be smashing dressed in white silk cut on the bias trimmed with maribou feathers!

Another simple guideline is that the groom's dress code is based upon time: the later the hour, the more formal his attire. Etiquette writers instructed that at a semiformal wedding, a tuxedo looks good at any time of the day, as does a dark business suit in winter and a light suit in summer. Certainly, at an informal wedding, a dark suit is perfect. Remember, it is a celebration of love that we're talking about. Rules can be relaxed. If you and your man were out picking mushrooms and the urge to marry came over you, no one would ever fault your romantic appearance in blue jeans and hiking boots.

But, back to wedding reality: In the case of a very formal daytime wedding and reception (bride with long train, elaborate sit-down dinner, big wedding party), if the groom wants to stay in a traditional key, he is advised to wear a black or oxford gray cutaway jacket, gray or beige waistcoat, black-and-gray-striped trousers, and a four-in-hand necktie, or ascot scarf.

A nighttime wedding always exudes an extra measure of excitement. Night, which is anytime after six, justifies full evening dress: black tailcoat with a white waistcoat and white bow tie. A boutonniere of stephanotis, lily of the valley, or white rose would be gorgeous on his lapel.

What if your fiancé has very definite, very individual fashion tastes? The groom, just like the bride, is free to roam the fields of fashion history, culling what he likes from the past. The range is enormous. He can choose to be dashing like Rhett Butler in a dark Victorian frock coat; as romantic as Lord Byron in a softly ruffled white shirt; as soignée as Beau Brummel in a beautifully tailored dark coat, buff-colored vest, and body-hugging trousers. A monacle might be all he needs to feel like Lord Peter Wimsey.

*A perfect Woman,
nobly plann'd,
To warn, to comfort,
and command;
And yet a Spirit still,
and bright
With something of
angelic light.*

WILLIAM WORDSWORTH:
*"She Was a Phantom of
Delight"*

Like the marriage of true minds, the groom's attire this day goes hand-in-hand with his bride's, the only exception being a military wedding. There, tradition dictates that if the groom wears a uniform, then the bride wears a long gown. A newer tradition dictates that if the bride is in the military and she opts to wear her dress uniform, then the groom is by her side in a dark suit or tuxedo. If both are in the service and decide to wear uniforms, then a whole lot of money has been saved!

Setting also helps determine the dress mood. What if you have found the most beautiful old yacht for your wedding? You'd look sensational in an off-the-shoulder chiffon gown with a large picture hat—and how about natty flannels and a blue blazer for the groom? Throw in a bright bow tie, and you've got a look Gatsby would have admired. Should your wedding take place in a glorious garden, match the delicate mood in hand-embroidered organdy. For the groom, there is nothing more elegant than a linen suit. Planning to dance the night away at a large reception to the lush sounds of a live orchestra? What could be more eye-catching than an exuberant "southern belle" satin gown as you twirl in the arms of your groom—who looks so dashing in a black frock coat with a softly ruffled shirt?

# · The Groomsmen ·

*W*hy is it that at most weddings, the groom and his ushers look like a chorus line? Because they are all dressed identically. This practice started as a ruse to confuse "evil" spirits as to who the happy groom actually was, thus avoiding any misfortune cast upon the bridal couple. Why this tradition has endured fits in nicely with the male psyche. Basically, men like to dress alike. They are devoted to uniforms: school, camp, sports, military, work. They are most comfortable when most alike. The gray flannel suit and the tuxedo are no accidents.

Of course, there are some grooms who don't fit this mold. They may want to make more of a statement and have their ushers and best man dress less conventionally. If this is what you want to do, it may take more time to put it together. Otherwise, if you decide to walk the more traditional path, and the need to rent formal wedding clothes arises, it is recommended that they be fitted and reserved far in advance—especially if you're marrying during a popular wedding month. One note of caution: If hats are to be worn, let the groom be forewarned that an old wedding superstition tells us it is unlucky for a hat to be dropped, or worse, lost!

## ·*The Bridal Attendants*·

*B*ecause they contribute so much to the gaiety and pa-gentry of the wedding, often, the true importance of the bridesmaids as trusted friends and allies is overlooked. There is no greater comfort for a bride to enter into this exciting change in her life than with the help of her brides-maids. Providing emotional support, wedding-decoration counseling, and best of all, candor, the bridesmaid has earned a place of honor in the wedding party. Arrayed in her special wedding clothes, she is part of the spectacle of the proces-sional. It's thrilling to see the bridemaids walking down the aisle, the emotion of the congregation ever escalating until the moment when the bride appears. If you plan to have a dozen—fine! If you lack ushers as escorts, bridesmaids, among their other talents, know how to walk down an aisle by themselves.

Once you decide on the composition of the wedding party (bridesmaids, junior bridesmaids, flower girls), the fun begins. The bride gets to decide what everybody will wear. Custom dictates that this is her prerogative, even though bridesmaids are expected to pay for their own gowns and shoes. This is part of the bridesmaid's gift to her friend.

The first question you may ask is: Why do bridesmaids

dress alike? Is this so the bride stands out? Originally, part of the bridesmaid's job description was to deflect the evil thought-rays of demons! Yes, this is something only a good friend would do. Rooted in the same superstition that has groom and groomsmen dressing alike, this tradition flourished until this century. Bridesmaids wore what the bride wore, sometimes even including a veil! When we look at etchings from women's magazines of the mid-1800s, such as *Godey's Lady's Book*, it's eerie to see the bride, covered from head to foot in white, surrounded by a group of identically dressed bridesmaids—almost like a ballet corps of brides. What confusion this must have made for guests! What expense for Papa!

Gradually, this superstition faded. The bride sought a solo in the spotlight. Arrayed in all her carefully selected finery, she became the show-stopper, her bridesmaids, satellites of her beauty. To enable the bride to stand out even more, bridesmaids still tend to dress in the same style, yet in different colors, providing a uniform backdrop for the delicate white of a bride's gown. Pastels as pretty as Easter candy have long dominated this fashion realm: sweet blues, peaches, light lemons, gentle grays, and lavender. Still, there is something very haunting and poetic about an all-white wedding. If you think this is something you would like to do, there are many beautiful shades of white from which to choose: buttercream, champagne, café au lait—they look as good as they sound!

When choosing bridesmaids' outfits, consider how they relate to your outfit. If yours is an informal country wedding and you plan to wear a simple dress yourself, then cotton frocks in French country florals, stripes, or paisleys couldn't be prettier for your attendants. Ruffled pinafores for the youngest bridal party members continue the sweet-as-strawberries atmosphere. Top them off with garlands of intense flowers such as bachelor buttons and black-eyed Susans.

What if you plan to celebrate with a glamorous evening reception? Keep a high pitch going and pull out all the stops. The groom and ushers look smashing in traditional white tie and tails. Your bridesmaids will love you forever if you dress them in shimmering taffeta, gold lamé, or silk charmeuse. These sumptuous fabrics make fabulous evening dresses your bridesmaids will be happy to wear again after the wedding. Pair them with bouquets that recall a slim-lined 1920s and 1930s elegance: camillias, gardenias, orchids, calla lilies. Sprays of these look gorgeous tucking up a fancy hairstyle or trailing through frothy curls.

How about the intimate wedding in a judge's chambers or justice-of-the-peace office, followed by a small reception?

You can still include as many bridal attendants as you like. Just because they're not walking down an aisle holding up a twenty-five-foot court train doesn't mean they are any less dear to you. The spirit and feeling of the day can be even more intense reflected off a smaller group of guests rather than a gathering of five hundred.

As at any wedding, the bride's outfit sets the tone and tenor. Exquisite silks, heirloom laces, or a linen suit are wonderful here. Create unity by asking your bridesmaids to dress in a certain color or period: nostalgic Gibson Girl blouses, luxurious cashmere sweaters, or silk blazers. Corsages of freesia or stephanotis streaming with the traditional blue-and-white knotted ribbons evoke the celebrations of our distant ancestors, the Elizabethans, who always wore gaily colored nosegays or wedding favours. These add a festive feeling as well as ensuring good luck for the bridal couple.

Present each attendant with a token of your affection—a small silver locket or heart. The sight of everyone wearing them is an emblem of togetherness certain to touch your heart this day.

One last word on bridesmaids: Bear in mind that bridesmaids are not scenery, but actual human beings. Empathize with their physically demanding roles, and consider the limits of their pocketbooks when selecting wardrobe. Hours of standing and dancing dictate that you forego three-inch spike heels. Show mercy by suggesting soft ballet slippers or even open-backed satin bedroom mules. Fussy, towering headpieces are trouble; opt instead for the elegance of simple wreaths, or upswept hairstyles caught with small nosegays.

## · F l o w e r   G i r l s ·

It is every girl's dream to be a flower girl. And if you know two, three, or four little girls you would like to make happy, please don't let anyone stop you. This is a centuries-old tradition especially revered by English royalty. If having more than one flower girl appeals to you, try to pair them by size and dress. At the informal wedding, they couldn't be prettier than when wearing cottons and linens. For evening, or for a very formal occasion, a heightened fanciness is called for, which little girls love. Floor-length organdies light as cotton candy are angelic; pretty ribbons around their hair and baskets of flowers in their arms are easy to manage. When Sarah Ferguson became the dutchess of York, her flower girls carried hoops entwined with blossoms for a look of English country romance at an ultraformal wedding held in Westminster Abbey.

## · *Hairstyles* ·

*B*rides are not the only ones guilty of fussing with their hairstyles. Grooms have traditionally devoted much time and thought to arranging their tresses: in long falls, ringlets, pompadours. It is only since the late nineteenth century that men have worn their hair short, with the exception of the great hair liberation of the 1960s—when the counterculture styles seemed to be a throwback to the days of long-haired pioneers and settlers. Now a groom can wear his hair in any style—but it is sensible for him to get a haircut a week or so before the wedding so that intervening days take the new edge off his look.

However, it is the bride's hair that traditionally has been charged with meaning, shrouded in myth and ancient traditions. Long ago, all young girls wore their hair long, flowing, and free, as a sign of innocence and youth. At her wedding, it was the custom for the bride's tresses to be unbound, covered only by a garland. After the wedding, a woman's hair was worn up or cut, as a signal of her new maturity, position, and unavailability. In the Middle Ages, the bride's hair would often be put up before the wedding feast. So potent a symbol was women's hair that in fifth-century-B.C. Sparta, the bride's hair was cut short like a man's. Furthering

*A woman can never be too fine while she is all in white.*

JANE AUSTEN

this transposition, the bride dressed in men's clothes. These drastic measures were taken to deflect the jealousy of any guests who otherwise might be tempted to kidnap a beautiful bride—before the honeymoon.

In the Orient, eyebrows are regarded as an intensely alluring feature of a woman's face. Long ago, after a traditional Chinese wedding, the bride's eyebrows were shorn entirely, rendering her powerless to attract men.

By the Victorian era, notions of simplicity were lost in a wealth of ornamentation. The bride's hair was rolled, curled, upswept, teased, braided. It was decorated with tassles, fringes, flowers, feathers, and jewels, all keeping perfect pace with the exuberantly decorated clothes of the day. This old-fashioned elegance may be perfect with your ensemble. Consider an upswept roll of hair fastened with a silver or faux ivory comb; a chignon encircled with lily of the valley; a cascade of ringlets pinned with sprays of white lilac; a halo of braids twisted with orange blossoms. They are all romantic and beautiful choices.

How lucky today's bride is, for she has little or no restrictions on her hairstyle. Free to choose what she wants, she harmonizes her style with the mood and formality of her wedding, and she does the same for her attendants. There is something so touching about young flower girls, their hair shiny and glowing, worn straight in a perfect Kate Greenaway cut, pulled up into top knots, or held back with velvet headbands. While traditionally very young flower girls have worn their hair loose, they look equally fetching with a more formal hairstyle—so long as it is not too sophisticated or glamorous.

## • D r e s s i n g   C e r e m o n i e s •

*A*n old European superstition warns the bride not to try on her complete bridal ensemble before the wedding, that it's bad luck to appear as the bride before the actual day. Since most wedding dresses used to be "Sunday best" topped with a borrowed veil, this wasn't too hard to heed. This superstition lingered even after brides had their wedding dresses custom-made. Princess Anne, at her first wedding in 1973, skirted this issue by decreeing that her seamstress leave a few stitches undone in her gown until the morning of her wedding.

Luck and superstition, mixed with respect for the past, seem to dominate the dressing ritual. In many Asian cultures, elaborate dressing ceremonies take hours, even days. While some Americans with strong ethnic ties still follow the traditions of their homelands, American brides have traditionally dressed with the assistance of their bridesmaids. Years ago, when brides married from their parents' homes, it was the custom for the bride to have her bridesmaids sleep over the night before the wedding. In Victorian times, even everyday dressing was a time-consuming chore, with corsets, chemises, underslips, bloomers, all having to be donned. So the extravagance of a wedding outfit needed more than usual care, and here was another way bridesmaids served a useful function. Besides, it was great fun. Dressing together is a charming custom that brings you closer to your friends, and if circumstances allow, it might be something you would want for your wedding.

As for the superstition that couples not see each other before arriving at the ceremony, this is something a modern lifestyle has not completely changed. Even when couples live together, many think it's fun to spend the night before the wedding apart so as to honor this old tradition.

*When love and skill work together expect a masterpiece.*

JOHN RUSKIN

## ''Something Old, Something New''

W hat is the best known of wedding adage/superstitions? Every schoolgirl knows this one:

# Wedding Day Dressing

SOMETHING OLD,

SOMETHING NEW,

SOMETHING BORROWED,

SOMETHING BLUE . . .

AND A SILVER SIXPENCE IN HER SHOE.

Even if brides think this is a silly superstition, there aren't too many who will ignore it. What is the significance of this advice? The *old* and the *new* represent rites of passage, something *old* being your link with the past. A lovely piece of family jewelry or the family Bible are especially appropriate. Something *new* represents the hope of success for the future. This could be your wedding dress, lingerie, or perhaps a strand of pearls from the groom. To *borrow* something from a dear friend is thought to borrow a bit of her good luck. The real tradition is to borrow something from a happily married friend. In the past, this was often a veil. And, something *blue* dates back to the days of the biblical Hebrews, for whom blue represented spiritual constancy and loyalty. Blue topaz earrings or light blue satin slippers are wonderful worn with white. As for the *silver sixpence* in your shoe, in America this translates to a silver dime. The coin, symbolizing future wealth, and the shoe, symbolizing authority, should impart some wisdom to the bride concerning women's roles and the need to keep one's fingers on the financial pulse of the marriage.

Staging a wedding can make you feel like a Broadway producer, costume designer, and magician all in one. There are so many elements to think about: dress, settings, entrances, and more. Every detail is significant—in particular, the look of the "cast members." If ever there was a time for pulling out all the stops and realizing your dreams, it's on your wedding day. Use this as a time to deepen your ties with your fiancé. Find a quiet nook, bring out a notebook, and jot down your thoughts and ideas about this extraordinary production!

*Chapter Nine*

# Wedding Flowers

ose petals float through the air, garlands crown happy brows, the bridal bouquet flies into the arms of the eager "next-to-marry." For centuries, the wedding has been a joyous ceremony glorified with a lavish use of flowers. Of all the wedding trimmings and flourishes, few stir the bride's senses more than her wedding flowers. Delicious scents dust the air as she moves toward the altar, fragile textured blooms nod from nosegays, the flowers from her bouquet brush against her hand. More than mere beauty though, flowers are highly charged symbols. From the bridal bouquet to the groom's boutonniere and the bridesmaids' garlands, down to the tiniest petals strewn by flower girls, every flower and herb holds within it a tale and a tradition.

Whether the bride is demure in a simple halo of baby's breath (thought to ensure a fruitful marriage) or dazzling in a crown of orange blossoms braided with diamonds (like Queen Victoria), she is arming herself with the power of two thousand years of tradition—traditions that are meant to ensure a fruitful marriage, that speak of the love between the bride and groom, that celebrate the continuity of life. So enduring a tradition are wedding flowers that many used in weddings today—roses, myrtle, orange blossoms, violets— trace their roots back to the gardens of the ancient Greeks and Romans. And one, the four-leaf clover, can be traced all the way back to the Garden of Eden, where it is believed that this good-luck symbol first appeared.

ONE LEAF FOR FAME,
AND ONE FOR WEALTH,
ONE FOR A FRUITFUL LOVER,
AND ONE TO BRING YOU GLORIOUS HEALTH
ARE IN A FOUR-LEAF CLOVER.

*Mattioli:*
COMMENTARIES

We look back to the ancient Greeks for the first records of wedding flora. But first, we have to understand that to early civilizations, harvest was the key to survival; the gifts of nature were to be revered. At their weddings, ancient Greeks took care to pay homage to nature's gifts by incorporating them into their celebrations. From head to foot, symbols of the harvest would grace the ceremony. Wreaths of grains—wheat, rye, oats—or herbs encircled the brows of the bridal couple. Paths strewn with wheat would cushion the bride's journey.

Fertility in all its forms was essential, but no more so than in human beings—childbearing. All early civilizations believed that marriage served a simple purpose: to have children. Children were considered a great blessing, necessity, and form of wealth. Thought to encourage fertility, young children were welcome participants in wedding celebrations. We see the very first "flower girls" in early Greek weddings. Young girls would precede the bride, carrying sheaves of freshly cut wheat to place upon the altar as a fertility offering. If the wedding took place out of season, gilded wheat would often be substituted for fresh—a look that is as elegant today as it was then. Mixed in with the grains would be other symbols of fertility: nuts and sweetmeats.

But the Greeks had a romantic side, too. As worshipers

of the goddess of love, they placed faith in the symbolic power of flowers, herbs, grains, and flowering trees to foster this wonderful feeling. Flowering quince, for instance, often decorated wedding festivals, because it was believed that the sharing of the fruit of the quince tree would increase the regard a couple had for each other.

## · W r e a t h s :  A  L o n g - l a s t i n g ·  B r i d a l  T r a d i t i o n

"With sweet-odored marjoram flowers, wreath thy beauty-radiant brow," wrote Catullus. To the ancient Greeks, it wasn't a wedding unless the bride wore a crown of flowers or leaves. If you seem preoccupied with your wedding flowers, rest assured that this has been true of brides for the past two thousand years. In fact, wreaths, circlets, garlands, or crowns worn on the head are one of the longest-standing continuous bridal traditions. As an unbroken circle, a wreath was viewed as a symbol of innocence for the bride. The Grecian bride had the dilemma of choosing among those made from violets, the symbol of purity and faith, or roses, myrtle, and the ever-important grains, among other options.

Long before Saint Valentine's Day came into being, the

ancient Greeks were intoxicated by the power of roses, find-ing love and desire to reside in the red rose, charm and innocence in the white. At weddings, both colors crowned the bride, sharing their beauty with her.

The Romans continued the tradition of the wedding wreath. Inspired by Venus, their goddess of love, Roman brides and grooms walked to the altar beneath a crown of flowers named the *corona nuptialis.* Besides the highly symbolic wreath of grain, a favored look was a braid of roses and marigolds, chosen for their associations with love and longevity.

The bridal wreath enjoys a happy old age; it lives on as beautiful as ever at weddings all over the world. In Norway, the bride is crowned with a wreath of white flowers; in Native-American ceremonies, maize encircles the bride's brow; flower girls in Great Britain still wear this traditional crown, a sign of sweet innocence.

## •*Strewing of Flowers* •

THE SHOWERS OF ROSES, LUCKY, FOURE-LEAV'D GRASSE,
THE WHILE THE CLOUD OF YOUNGLINGS SING,
AND DROWN YE WITH A FLOWRIE SPRING.

*Robert Herrick:*
HESPERIDES

*I*t's surprising to realize that almost since weddings began, brides have been walking on more than air on their way to the altar. The strewing of the bridal path with grains, herbs, flowers, or rushes was an important tradition, thought to help bring fertility and prosperity to the married couple.

Many centuries ago, young children, their arms laden with grains, would set out to cover the bride's path to the ceremony. Herbs were often mixed in: lemon-scented balm, the symbol of sympathy and love, and mint, the plant of Jupiter (and a rampant grower) released their scents as the bride trod over them. If you are to be married in a garden, perhaps you would like to have your path to the marriage site strewn in this charming fashion by your flower girls or ring bearers.

ALL DEAR NATURE'S CHILDREN SWEET,
LIE 'FORE THE BRIDE AND BRIDEGROOM'S FEET.

*J. Fletcher:*
TWO NOBLE KINSMEN

In Elizabethan England, it became the fashion to scent one's home. Lacking chemical air fresheners, the resourceful Elizabethans turned to the next-best thing, nature. Every day, floors were strewn with rushes or hay. On a wedding day, special flowers such as rose petals and herbs lent their heady aromas to the bridal potpourri. This lovely custom of walking "on a bed of roses" must have felt wonderful for the bride, as she literally absorbed the bounty and beauty of nature from the foot up. While today's bride does not always have a carpet of flowers at her command, many brides continue to walk down the aisle on a trail of rose petals, strewn by flower girls, an exquisite tradition that generations past might be gratified to know still lives on. And, often, as today's bridal couple leaves the ceremony site, they are showered with rose petals, reenacting another ancient rite of love.

## · The Orange Blossom: · One Powerful Symbol

Why is it that orange blossom is still so identified with weddings? Probably few of us have actually seen an orange blossom, much less know the reasons behind the tradition. But of all wedding flowers dating back to antiquity that have a powerful hold on the bride's heart, surely none is more renowned than orange blossom. Century after century of brides have incorporated this legendary flower into their bridal ensembles, and it remains an unshakable motif in the wedding canon.

Its origins enshrined in myth, orange blossom was first associated with the Greek goddess Hera, who married Zeus, King of Heaven. Ancient myth holds that Hera was presented with orange blossoms by Gaea, the goddess of earth and fertility, on her wedding night. It's interesting to note that the goddess Hera is responsible for the concept of a marriage "being made in heaven," as Greek marriages were celebrated before offerings to this divine goddess.

Juno, the Roman Queen of Heaven and protector of women and marriage, also received orange blossoms when she married Jupiter, the supreme deity of the Roman gods,

*We are shaped and fashioned by what we love.*

JOHANN WOLFGANG VON GOETHE

another marriage made in heaven (although some historians believe it was the other way around, with Juno giving Jupiter the orange blossoms). Further enhancing the aura of this mythic flower is the belief that the golden fruit from the Garden of Hesperides was, in fact, the orange.

Apart from myth and legend, there are compelling botanical reasons why orange blossoms claim an enduring place as a symbol of fertility and love. The orange tree has the unique ability to bloom in all seasons and to bear fruit at the same time that it flowers. In addition, it's an evergreen, never shedding its leaves, always vibrant and alive, much as a successful marriage should be.

European brides in the Middle Ages were also captivated

by orange blossoms. In their day, its appearance was credited to no less a holy force than the Crusaders. Legend has it that as Crusaders returned from the East, they glimpsed Saracen brides wearing beautiful white orange blossoms in their hair. So moved were the warriors by the sight of this loveliness that they brought back orange-tree cuttings to root in their own home soil. Whether or not this actually happened is the stuff of myth, but we do know that orange trees were planted in the royal gardens at Versailles in the sixteenth century, and soon thereafter, English landscape designers made a space for them in their own gardens. In China, orange blossoms are revered both as a symbol of purity and as a harbinger of good luck.

But it was a twenty-year-old queen who brought back the orange-blossom tradition for modern times. When young Queen Victoria, who could choose from her vast collection of priceless diamond tiaras to hold her wedding veil, chose instead a wreath of orange blossoms for her hair, a signal went out that Victoria wished to be married as a woman, not as a monarch. This bow to romantic tradition instantly captured the hearts of brides on both sides of the Atlantic, and orange blossoms became firmly rooted in Victorian-era bridal repertoire. Ever since that time, Windsor brides have taken care to tuck an orange blossom in their bridal ensemble. When the present queen mother was married in 1923, she wore an orange-blossom motif. This valiant bride carried a bouquet of white roses and heather, which she had the heart to place on the grave of the Unknown Warrior at Westminster Abbey before walking up the aisle with her prayer book in hand.

By the turn of the twentieth century, Americans had already read about their own leading families carrying on this tradition. When Nellie Grant, the beautiful daughter of President Ulysses S. Grant, married in 1874, masses of orange blossoms along with lilies and roses decked the East Room in one of the most opulently decorated weddings ever held in the White House. In 1906, Alice Roosevelt, eldest daughter of President Theodore Roosevelt, also married in the White House. She wore a tulle veil caught up with orange blossoms and carried a bouquet of orchids. In another famous wedding, closer to our time, in 1968, Jacqueline Kennedy and Aristotle Onassis adorned themselves with orange blossoms at their ceremony.

Because the extravagant cost of real orange blossoms was out of the reach of all but a few well-to-do, many Victorian brides substituted silk, paper, or wax versions of the blossoms. These artificial creations in turn created their own superstition—that of discarding them within one month of the wedding—presumably the end of the lifespan of a real orange blossom.

It's interesting to note that one of the reasons put forth for the popularity of velvety stephanotis as a wedding flower is thought to be its resemblance to orange blossoms and its relative low cost.

## • M y r t l e •

The Ancient Greeks believed that life-enhancing qualities existed in flowers, herbs, and greens, qualities which they hoped could be imparted to the bride and groom. They especially loved the fragrant evergreen myrtle. Greek myth describes how Aphrodite, the goddess of love and beauty, emerged from the ocean accompanied by nereids or sea nymphs carrying wreaths of dark, glossy-leaved myrtle. Thus myrtle was seen as a perfect lovers' flower. And, because it could bloom year-round, it was associated with the constancy of love.

Centuries later, Queen Victoria wove myrtle into her bridal bouquet along with snowdrops, the favorite flower of her beloved bridegroom, Prince Albert. This in turn started a charming tradition of its own in the British royal family, as cuttings from this same myrtle spray were planted in the royal gardens on the Isle of Wight following Queen Victoria's wedding. Subsequent generations of Windsor brides have carried cuttings from this wellspring of marital bliss to honor the deep love that so influenced Victoria.

Country folk had beliefs about the powers of myrtle as well. It was a custom in eighteenth-century England for a bridesmaid to plant myrtle on either side of the newlyweds' cottage—one side representing the bride, the other, the groom. If the myrtle took root, it was believed that the bridesmaid herself would enjoy marital happiness. Should the plant ever flower, it was said to be extra-lucky, as myrtle is a plant that requires skill to bring to bloom.

It's certainly a lovely idea to carry a wedding bouquet with a plant that can be rooted later. Ivy is an ideal choice, for it, too, is a wedding symbol, and its sure-rootedness is much like a successful marriage itself—always growing and difficult to disturb.

## · Wedding Decorations of · Herbs and Flowers

*T*he instinct to decorate the wedding site—be it an altar, a *huppah*, a mahogany sideboard at home, or an arbor in a beautiful garden—is as ancient as the wedding itself. Since antiquity, brides have busied themselves preparing for the wedding. Garlands and ropes braided with flowers crowned door frames and arches; sheaves of wheat stood as sentinels at doorways; fresh flowers, fruits, herbs, and vegetables were arranged on altars much as they are today. Lacking the services of a professional floral designer, the bride and the female members of her family used nature's bounty to decorate with everything in bloom: pussy willows in late winter; apple and cherry blossoms in spring; fragrant flowers in summer; autumn leaves after the harvest; holly and yew in early winter.

*Flowers of all hue, and without thorn the rose.*

JOHN MILTON:
*Paradise Lost*

To the Victorians, too much was never enough: Wedding bells of carnations, roses, and chrysanthemums hung over arches to frame the bridal couple; tables bloomed with runners of roses and ferns; potted palms banked every corner. The joy of wedding festivities was heightened even further by these festive decorations—a custom that still entrances brides today as they plan altar and pew decorations, flowers for their hair, and garlands for the reception.

## · *The Bride's Bouquet* ·

*A*part from reasons associated with fertility, early Grecian brides carried handfuls of herbs and grains to deter any jealous spirits lurking about the ceremony. It has been a persistent superstition that the display of too much happiness or good fortune will be punished by the evil eye, so since ancient times, brides have been arming themselves with protective shields: their wedding bouquets. Elizabethan brides made sure to include garlic and chives, notorious for their aromatic qualities—perhaps deterring a jealous guest or two at the same time!

Other sweeter additions to the bride's bouquet might include mint and marigold to heighten amorous feelings, sesame and parsley to increase fertility, and sweet basil to inspire good luck.

In the Middle Ages, agriculture began to diversify from strictly utilitarian crops as families became more affluent. Cuttings of plants from newly explored parts of the world were brought to the great European gardens for planting. And the interest in cultivating new garden flowers exploded.

New ways to use them were found just as quickly. The more affluent could indulge their taste for the exotic, and the wedding was the perfect place to show off all these flowers.

At the same time, bridal fashion was evolving away from heavily decorating wedding sites and began to center more and more on the bride, as most brides would agree it should.

The bridal bouquet, for centuries a loosely tied clutch of lucky herbs, greens, and wildflowers, was transformed into a formal arrangement dominated by cultivated flowers. This bouquet was christened the *nosegay,* a word from Middle English that literally meant something pretty for the nose to smell, especially comforting during an emotional time. The nosegay, a diminutive, round mound of flowers, is such a captivating style that it has remained a bridal tradition for over four hundred years.

Also in the Elizabethan era, the concept of romantic love raged full blown in the imaginations of poets and sensitive lovers. Flowers, invested with personalities and powers of their own, became symbols of this love. For the first time, the bride made artful bouquets from flowers based upon their romantic associations. Lily of the valley, wild carrot (or Queen Anne's lace), roses, pansies, violets, and baby's breath were great favorites.

## · The Groom's Flowers ·

*A*s a nervous groom pins a white rose onto his lapel just before the service, he can take comfort in knowing that this small act links him to countless generations of bridegrooms who have worn flowers before him. It is another instance of the many ways that the hope for fertility has been expressed.

Roman grooms were crowned with wreaths. Later, nosegays that fastened onto elaborate wedding finery were provided for men at Elizabethan weddings. For the Victorians, boutonnieres were a mainstay of the groom's attire, usually of a flower from the bride's bouquet. The Edwardian groom fancied gardenias, despite their pronounced fragrance.

All the male members of the wedding party are similarly decorated, and for a time it was the fashion to wear the flower blossoms downward so as to keep them fresh.

## · R o s e m a r y ·

"*I*t is an herbe sacred to rememberance, and therefore to friendship," wrote Sir Thomas More. And indeed, were the bride sitting at a Tudor wedding feast, more than likely the buttery scent of rosemary would be wafting through the air. If she looked underfoot, the floor was probably strewn with it. A silver wine goblet would be holding a sprig wrapped in gay ribbons to sweeten the posset the bride and groom would share. Dozens of small nosegays, gilded and tied with colored ribbons, would be ready to give out to guests.

Of all the herbs that have come to symbolize marriage, rosemary is one that should have a special place in lovers' hearts. For this shrubby herb, with its warm, soothing scent, is legendary for having the power to strengthen memory. As memory is such an important part of fidelity, we can see how it became an emblem for lovers.

The love affair with rosemary began early. Sprigs of rosemary, dipped in sweetened water, appeared at Roman marriage ceremonies. Bushes of rosemary are said to have sheltered the Virgin Mary on her flight into Egypt.

The Elizabethans adored rosemary and devised many different ways to incorporate it into daily life, as well as wedding festivities. "It is surnamed coronaria . . . because women have been accustomed to make crowns and garlands thereof," wrote the great botanist John Gerard in *The Herball*, in 1597. By the sixteenth century, garden writings contained many recipes for rosemary as an ingredient in foods, ointments, and perfumes.

*An ideal wife is any woman who has an ideal husband.*

BOOTH TARKINGTON:
*Looking Forward to the Great Adventure*

FOR YOU THERE'S ROSEMARY AND RUE; THESE KEEP
SEEMING AND SAVOUR ALL THE WINTER LONG.

*William Shakespeare:*
THE WINTER'S TALE

Elizabethan brides thought it would bring luck to wear sprigs of rosemary on their wedding day; in fact, in 1540, Anne of Cleves, the fourth wife of Henry VIII, was married wearing a gold coronet encircled with sprigs of rosemary. (This, unfortunately, was one instance where herbal powers were not able to help save a disastrous marriage; they were divorced the same year.)

The romantic Elizabethans would also celebrate at their wedding feasts seated under "kissing knots," ribbons tucked with croton leaves and rosemary, then suspended above the bridal couple. Another sweet custom was for friends of the bride to present the groom with a small nosegay of rosemary, a subtle reminder of their expectations.

## · The Victorian Language · of Flowers

The Victorian era did more than inspire wedding fashions. Family values and women's role in controlling them was increasing in importance. During the six decades of Victoria's reign, nearly every aspect of social behavior came under intense scrutiny—particularly courtship and weddings. Perhaps because of this, elaborate codes that substituted for open discourse sprang up among courting people.

Calling cards became virtual encyclopedias of meaning, the use of fans nearly required an on-the-spot translator. But nowhere was there a greater vocabulary of hidden meanings than in the language of flowers. So obsessed were the Victorians with flowers that one could only imagine the riotous cacophony that would have resulted if flowers had possessed actual voices.

Everyone, from ministers to poets, had his or her own notion of what flowers were actually saying. *The Language of Flowers*, illustrated by Kate Greenaway and still so beloved today, was but one popular guide to the intricacies of floral language. Were a Victorian lady to receive a bouquet of pansies from a suitor, she could quickly decode that he was asking her to "think of me," since the word pansy comes from the French *pensée*, meaning thought or sentiment. Should she be sent a double red pink, she learned it signified pure love, while a variegated pink sent in return signaled refusal. Lilacs were translated to mean first love, and lilies, purity. Roses were the most fluent flowers of all, expressing several different sentiments at once. Their color, length, even whether or not their thorns were removed had a meaning for the highly semantic Victorians. Red roses conveyed desire, white roses, innocence. Yellow presaged jealousy—perhaps that is why we see so few yellow flowers at weddings.

LOVE'S LANGUAGE MAY BE
TALKED WITH THESE;
TO WORK OUT CHOICEST
SENTENCES
NO BLOSSOM CAN BE MEETER;

AND, SUCH BEING USED IN
EASTERN BOWERS,
YOUNG MAIDS MAY WONDER
IF THE FLOWERS
OR MEANINGS BE THE
SWEETER.

*Elizabeth Barrett Browning*

In their relentless quest for meaning, the Victorians also aligned certain flowers to months of the year, much as gems became birthstones. Including them in bridal bouquets was considered another way to evoke marital good luck.

| | |
|---|---|
| *January* | *snowdrop* |
| *February* | *primrose* |
| *March* | *jonquil* |
| *April* | *sweet pea* |
| *May* | *lily of the valley* |
| *June* | *rose* |
| *July* | *larkspur* |

| *August* | *poppy* |
| *September* | *morning glory* |
| *October* | *cosmos* |
| *November* | *chrysanthemum* |
| *December* | *holly* |

With all of these guidelines, Victorian brides had a lot to think carefully about in selecting their bridal flowers. To them, preparation and participation were twin virtues. There were few ways to record the on-the-spot action, the invention of the camcorder being over a hundred years away, so brides devoted much energy to the meanings and rituals that would make the wedding memorable.

Given their enthusiasm for flowers, it's no surprise that the Victorians also created new forms of bouquets. The tiny nosegay became the tussie-mussie, a somewhat larger, round bouquet, now held in its own horn-shaped holder. Highly sought-after antiques today, some tussie-mussie holders were designed to stand on the reception table and keep the bridal flowers fresh. Circlets and horseshoes of flowers were charming alternatives, especially for brides-maids and flower girls.

The turn of the twentieth century ushered in the advent of the elaborate wedding gown frosted with tucking, ruching, pleating, tassels, and fringe. Larger bouquets were needed for balance. The tussie-mussie grew into the chatelaine. Round and plump as a leg-of-mutton sleeve, the chatelaine featured a cluster of flowers, usually white, circled by ferns.

In another innovation, the chatelaine or tussie-mussie would contain the letters of a precious word, or the couple's initials in the center. President Grant's daughter Nellie carried a bouquet of tuberoses and orange blossoms with a silver inset in the center spelling the word LOVE.

Like a Virginia creeper, once the bridal bouquet started to grow, it could not stop. Soon, the chatelaine had transformed itself into the show-stopping shower bouquet or cascade. Living up to its name, this was a wildly extravagant display of flowers. Massive, expensive, and the new favorite of royalty, dozens of flowers flowed down to a tapering point, often brushing the floor. Cascades were composed of dazzling white hothouse blooms—gardenias, orchids, lilac, calla lilies, tulips, freesia, hyacinths, stephanotis, orange blossoms—placed on a backdrop of ivy or other trailing greens.

Two trend-setting weddings of the British aristocracy in the 1890s firmly established this lavish bridal bouquet as a desirable style. In 1893, when Princess Victoria Mary of Teck married the duke of York (who later became King

George V), she carried a glorious arrangement of white carnations, House of York white roses, orchids, lily of the valley, and the royal favorite, orange blossoms. Two years later, in a wedding that came to characterize the marriage of American money to British nobility, Consuelo Vanderbilt, heiress to the vast American Vanderbilt fortunes, was united with the duke of Marlborough. Her sprawling bouquet of white orchids and lily of the valley was outlined with ferns.

The durability of the cascade as a statement bouquet was seen more recently in royal weddings. In 1981, Princess Diana's stupendous cascade of dozens of white roses gave her something enormously heavy to carry down the aisle, perhaps distracting her from the televised spectacle that British royal weddings have become.

In another royal wedding, Sarah Ferguson married Prince Andrew in 1986 carrying a long trailing bouquet of lily of the valley, cream roses, gardenias, and lilies. According to the floral designer who created her bouquet, the dutchess-to-be did not wish to have any greenery in her bouquet. This was an unfortunate oversight; Victorian brides often included sprigs of ivy, because ivy when rooted is difficult to disturb, much as a happy marriage should be.

In 1973, at her first wedding, Princess Anne carried a

bouquet of white roses, orchids, stephanotis, lily of the valley, and a sprig of myrtle harvested from that long-ago myrtle carried by Queen Victoria.

## • L o v e   K n o t s   o f   R i b b o n •

M any brides continue the lovely tradition of ribbons with "love knots" tied in them. Streaming from the poetic nosegay, the cascade bouquet, or chatelaine, long satin ribbons do more than look pretty: knotted, they are thought to bring good luck to the marriage. Traditionally, three knots are said to represent the bride, groom, and future children. Sometimes dozens of knots are tied in the ribbons, each entwined with a rosebud or other dainty flower. Jessica Wilson, the daughter of President Woodrow Wilson, carried a huge bouquet of roses streaming with knots at her White House wedding. As an extra wedding favour, the ribbons were cut into tiny pieces and distributed to guests, especially unmarried members of the wedding party, as tokens of marital good luck.

## • B e y o n d   A r t   D e c o   E l e g a n c e •

T he contemporary bride who selects a bouquet of creamy, elegant calla lilies has much in common with her sisters in spirit from the 1920s. Recalling the long, slim lines of gowns of shimmering fabrics, these flowers were every bit a match for art deco elegance and were the flower of choice for the flapper era. Carrying a single stem or flowers of all one type was particularly soigné.

Because of stringent wartime rationing, the bride of the 1940s was forced to be as resourceful about her wedding flowers as she was about gathering the ingredients for her wedding cake. Farmers turned their flower meadows to vegetable fields, and home gardens became Victory Gardens. The summer bride could hope for rambling roses and wildflowers, perhaps the forerunner of today's natural look. But more often, the patriotic bride made her own flowers out of fabrics or paper. Pressed and framed like real blooms, many of these have become cherished family heirlooms.

Perhaps because of wartime thriftiness, a custom that sprang up in the United States in the late 1940s and 1950s was that of making the bridal bouquet do double duty. A corsage, usually made with the enormously popular white orchid, was inserted in the middle of the bouquet. After the reception, the corsage was removed and pinned on by the new bride before departing for her honeymoon. However, not everyone approved of this custom. In her 1947 book *Wedding Etiquette Complete*, Marguerite Bentley firmly steered the bride-to-be away from this option, contending that not only would her corsage risk being crushed in the passion of the day, but that the bridal bouquet, sans the corsage, made an unsightly trophy to throw at eager bridesmaids!

## • *Flower Children* •

*W*e still remember the contribution of the 1960s and 1970s to weddings, because that fresh-from-the-meadow look remains so popular. Daisy chains, daffodil, anemone, primrose, Queen Anne's lace, sweet William—every type of uncomplicated garden bloom became a part of the country wedding feeling. Brides seemed to be reaching for a simpler ideal, with almost an artless feeling that is usually the result of greater sophistication. Today, we see this carried out in the "English country bouquet," a deceptively casual arrangement that captures the hushed beauty of well-tended perennial gardens.

## • *Tossing the Bride's Bouquet* •

*A*s the bride leaves the wedding reception, there is one last tradition: the tossing of the bridal bouquet. Standing on a chair or staircase, the bride turns her back and gives a mighty throw. Hands fly up as passionately as they would to catch a ball hit into the grandstands at a World Series game. It's almost a guarantee that the lucky person who catches it will be the next to marry! While earlier in this century the bouquet was thrown only to unmarried bridesmaids, nowadays, it is the custom to invite everyone to have a chance at catching it, even gentlemen friends who wish to marry.

There was a lovely Victorian tradition of making up a bridal bouquet consisting of several smaller bouquets which the bride could dismantle and toss before departing. In another tradition, the bride, reluctant to part with a keepsake as precious as her bouquet, made a secret "toss" bouquet to substitute for the real one at the right moment. Whether this stand-in bouquet was as effective at promoting marital luck is a matter of pure speculation.

The tossing of the bouquet is one of those bridal customs that is clearly traceable to fourteenth- and fifteenth-century England. There, amid another bridal custom of bedding the couple on the wedding night, young male friends of the groom would dash at the bride as she took to the bed, hoping to grab hold of her garter as a trophy. Soon, the bride's friends and family, also present in the crowded bridal chamber, saw an opportunity for sport and joined in the melee.

As a means of self-preservation, brides learned to tear off their own garters quickly and throw them at the boisterous assemblage. As weddings became more "civilized" in the eighteenth century, the bride was still expected to toss something. The bridal bouquet was ideal. While some brides and grooms continue the tradition of tossing garters to male guests, it is still the bridal bouquet that is considered the real catch.

## · Today's Flowers ·

*T*hroughout history, brides have always adorned themselves—be it with gilded wheat, myrtle, orange blossoms, chives and thyme, the white rose of the Yorks, or their favorite childhood bloom. Across time and across continents, brides always hope that flowers will bring them luck. To the poetic Japanese bride, a bouquet picked in the snow by a maiden friend is about as wonderful a way to start her marriage as she could hope to have.

The forms of floral adornment vary. The bride may carry a delicate nosegay of violets and lace, and feel like an Edwardian lady. She may enter a cathedral with an enormous armful of imported cattleya orchids, or stop by a meadow on her way to a country chapel to gather bachelor buttons and black-eyed Susans. A crown of myrtle and orange blossoms may be the royal family tradition, while a prayer book covered with lily of the valley may be what every bride in her family has carried. Virtually any choice she makes connects to the past and enriches her bridal experience. And her choice will be right; for as she leaves the wedding site, she might want to remember these poetic thoughts:

THE RING IS ON MY HAND,
AND THE WREATH IS ON MY BROW,
SATINS AND JEWELS GRAND
ARE ALL AT MY COMMAND,
AND I AM HAPPY NOW.

*Edgar Allan Poe*

# Chapter Ten

# The Marriage Ceremony

. . . FOR FAIRER OR FOULER, FOR BETTER OR WORSE,

FOR RICHER OR POORER . . .

*Old Anglo-Saxon wedding vow*

do." Letter for letter, these are probably the two most compelling words in the English language. They have the ability to change one's life. The vow of commitment has been the heart of the wedding ceremony since betrothals began. But before these two beautiful words are spoken, the bride and groom have a spectrum of joyful decisions to make. There are sites to view, vows to write, processionals to plan, and many wonderful wedding traditions to explore.

Deciding to get married is hard enough. Now you have to determine how you want to marry and who will marry you. It was a mere four hundred years ago that couples married themselves. Now, marriage can be a religious vow blessed by a clergyperson, or a civil service administered by a judge. At its most basic, marriage is a contract governed by the state. Many options exist for you besides the traditional clergyperson presiding in a house of worship. Does an outdoor service excite you? How about a trip back in time to your favorite childhood chapel and old family minister? Have you always envisioned a *huppah* set up in Grandmother's rose beds? Or a wedding at a famous old mansion?

Take time over this decision, because it is an important one. On a spiritual level, it links you with both the past and the future. On a practical level, you want a setting where as little as possible can go wrong! A seaside reception is lovely—except in a downpour. Open skies are peaceful—far from an airport. The town pond is special—but not when geese have been nesting there. It's easy to see why most couples opt for the indoor wedding.

The outdoor wedding enjoyed a rousing revival during the 1960s and 1970s. Amid long tables laden with homemade wedding cakes and pies, enveloped by the sweet notes of fiddle players, couples exchanged handwritten vows waist-high in meadows of wildflowers, along sun-drenched beaches, beside cherished old ponds. The rustic simplicity of the counterculture may fast be developing into a museum piece, but the allure of the outdoor wedding is still strong. Certainly, it is hard to imagine a more gracious setting than a family home with rolling lawns and freshly starched linens swaying in a June breeze.

This leads us to the topic of the at home wedding, which has enjoyed a long and prestigious history in our country. As recently as the nineteenth century, most weddings in America were still held at home. This custom was in part a holdover from the old days when settlers lived miles apart. Celebrations brought these rugged people together, often for days, so everyone enjoyed the opportunity to visit. The other contributing factor was that our early European settlers were Puritans, who did not feel the church had a place in what they believed was essentially a civil contract. But there was an even earlier group: Native Americans were famous for their hospitality, and many North American Indian tribes celebrated weddings "at home."

The at-home wedding is a sentimental favorite that continues to exert its considerable charm on a new generation of brides. Perhaps because you are surrounded by all that is dear and known, perhaps because you've always seen yourself

*True love's the gift which God has given To man alone beneath the heaven.*

Sir Walter Scott:
*The Lay of the Last Minstrel*

coming down the stairway on Father's arm, the at-home wedding delivers a profound emotional impact. It has plus points on a practical level, too. There is no need for transportation for the bridal party to a wedding site, which gives the bride greater control in terms of dress and preparation. One note of caution: An at-home wedding can equal and surpass the costs of one at a hotel, banquet hall, country club, or restaurant, especially when the guest list is large and elaborate catering and tent rentals are factored in.

## · H u p p a h s ·

T he beauty and power of the wedding service are part of the legacy of the ancient Jewish religion, and the tradition of the outdoor wedding has long been part of its heritage. With their roots deep in biblical times, Jewish weddings were once held under the shelter of a full *huppah*, a four-sided cloth canopy rich in symbolism. Among its many meanings, the *huppah* is seen as a sanctuary for bride and groom, a symbol of the new couple's home, and foremost, a spiritual haven blessed by God.

Each corner of the *huppah* was held aloft over the bridal couple by a male member of the congregation. Later, this evolved into the custom of tying each side to a pole to create a small tentlike shelter. Because a *huppah* can be anything from the simplest plain cloth to an elaborately embroidered and decorated canopy, held on high by tree branches or entwined with favorite vines and flowers, it can become exactly what the bridal couple envisions for this day.

Coverage as a form of protection exists in many cultures: In Scandinavia and France, square pieces of cloth are sometimes held over the bride and groom; in China, an old lady holds an umbrella over the bride's head; nineteenth-century Hindu weddings took place under canopies; and in Russian Orthodox ceremonies, the bride and groom stand under crowns held by attendants. Armenian couples married by priests would take part in a beautiful ceremony where their heads were crowned with flowers and gold ribbons. The priest tied the ribbons together, saying, "I unite you and bind you together. Live in peace."

## • Decorating the Site •

N ow that you have decided where to marry, the next consideration will be a fun one: how to decorate the site. For if nature abhors a vacuum, so does a floral designer. Weddings are rich in the tradition and symbolism of flowers, and this day calls for lavish displays, whether they be masses of seasonal flowers, cuttings from flowering trees, or your favorite hothouse blooms.

Great pots of quince, cherry blossoms, or dogwood make a springtime wedding memorable when placed on the altar or around the base of a *huppah*. Cuttings of holly and ivy look spectacular at winter weddings, as do buckets blazing with branches of fiery colored leaves in the autumn. Ropes of herbs and seasonal blooms hark back to Shakespearean times when young brides swagged them over doorways and arches.

You'll find so many exciting ways to use flowers, just as Victorian brides did: Line front steps with buckets of freshly picked garden flowers; hang baskets of posies from doorknobs and chair backs; recreate a favorite Victorian-style setting of wicker trellis and palms. The turn-of-the-century bride went all out with great displays. Especially dear to her heart were traditional wedding symbols fashioned from fresh flowers: hearts, knots, rings, and the large, oversize wedding bell. Usually composed of white mums and roses, the wedding bell would hang from a doorway or a trellis especially set up for the wedding. If married at home, most likely the Victorian maiden would have a low platform erected at the far end of a room. Covered with an Oriental rug, this is where the clergyman stood with bride and groom to perform the service.

So many decorative ideas await you, from simple to elaborate. Just be sure that when planning your decorations you take a long look at your site from different angles, in different lights, to see how it will photograph, especially on videotape. Beauty this special must be recorded, but you don't want your faces obscured or shadowed by your decorations. One additional note of caution: Before doing anything, check with your floral designer or someone in charge at the wedding site just to be sure your ideas are permitted.

## · The Procession ·

THE BLITHESOME, BUCKSOME, COUNTRY MAIDS,
WITH KNOTS OF RIBBANDS AT THEIR HEADS,
AND PINNERS FLUTTERING IN THE WIND,
THAT FAN BEFORE, AND TOSS BEHIND.

*Edward Chicken:*
"THE COLLIER'S WEDDING"

*T*he wedding procession actually begins before the walk down the aisle. In the past, the procession began as the couple traveled to the wedding site. This was an important tradition. As noted earlier, our ancient ancestors took care to protect the soon-to-be-wed from any harm. Any number of unpleasant incidents were waiting to strike—lightning, a sudden storm, a wild and hungry animal. So an "honor guard" formed to shelter the bride and groom. And what started off as a custodial function has evolved today into the stretch limousine, also a form of protection, if you will.

As far back as the early Greeks and Romans, a bride was escorted to her wedding site cosseted in a phalanx of ten women friends, often by torchlight to dispel evil spirits. As centuries and civilizations passed, the bride and groom set out together, usually on foot, in the company of friends and neighbors. In a merry band, they tramped across meadow and field, adding more and more well-wishers as their walk went on.

Later, in medieval times, the procession was very colorful. Minstrels preceded the couple, filling the air with music and song, all the more bawdy after the marriage. Flower girls carefully carried the bride's cup, filled with rosemary to symbolize remembrance. At the head of the gay procession, children took the lead as ever-important symbols of fertility. The bride was sandwiched between two unmarried male escorts, her "bridegrooms." Young maidens, or bridesmaids, followed, carrying garlands of wheat and bride's cakes.

The wedding procession has varied from culture to culture: Ancient Chinese bore their brides off in sedan chairs; Turkish brides often rode on horseback inside a canopy; German brides, ever romantic, arrived in a white coach to

symbolize good luck; ancient Hebrew brides arrayed themselves inside canopied litters; country brides in England often
rode in a pony and trap. The common thread among all was
the fear of touching the ground before the ceremony. It was
a strong belief among ancients that jealous demons inhabited
the ground and that it would be bad luck to brush up against
them on one's wedding day.

## · Why Does the Bride Stand at · the Groom's Left Side When Taking Her Vows?

W hen you take your vows, you may not realize it,
but if you stand to your groom's left as women
have done for thousands of years, you are helping to protect
yourself from any would-be marauders. One reason given for
the bride's standing on that side is that as most people are
right-handed, the groom would have needed to keep his right
arm free in order to defend his woman.

## · The Horse-drawn Carriage ·

W hile we may not have the above worries today,
except for the at-home wedding, most brides and

grooms still like to travel to their ceremony in something fancy and special. We've all seen convoys of rented limousines pulling up outside churches and synagogues. They are lots of fun, but you may also want to consider walking in an old-fashioned procession, if the ceremony is nearby. Or you could be ultraromantic and arrive in a horse-drawn carriage. If you do this, don't forget the traditional nosegays of white knotted ribbons on the horses' ears, and be sure to pin a nosegay on the driver as well. British royalty always dust off their famous "glass" carriage to bear the Windsor brides to Westminster Abbey, and if the weather is lovely, the happy couple rides in an open-air carriage on the way back. An old superstition advises that a carriage pulled by a gray horse will bring extra good luck.

## ·The Beginning of the Wedding· Party: The Best Man

*I*n ancient times, when maidens were snatched from their homes, did the bold "grooms" pull off these daring deeds by themselves? No, a man had a sidekick riding shotgun when stealing a wife. That is the dubious origin of one of the oldest of all marital traditions, the "best man." Much more than a good buddy who comforted the groom's jittery nerves, this brave ally created ruses and distractions while the groom ensnared his prey. Since abduction was considered marriage, this early groomsman's role was also the start of another wedding tradition—he was the first witness to the new couple's being joined as man and wife. The word "groom" itself is credited to a later era, when the wedding had become more civilized. At the wedding feast, the new husband served food and drink to his wife, "attending" her much as a groom would.

Occasionally, a groom felt expansive enough to compensate the bride's father for the loss of his property; then, the best man acted as a proxy for the groom, who understandably kept his distance. Later, as more and more marriages were financial arrangements not involving kidnapping, the best man's role took on a diplomatic dimension as he interceded between the two families. After having successfully completed the negotiations, he then provided another service: escorting the bride to her new home, protecting her from abduction by somebody else along the way.

Even after marriage-by-capture vanished from everyday practice after the Middle Ages, it left behind a custom in the British countryside of a mock "capture" in which the bride and groom were pursued on horseback by male members of the bride's family.

## · At the Wedding ·

O nce you've gotten to the ceremony, the processional usually forms in the vestibule. How you proceed down to the altar is entirely up to you. The old English wedding processional was colorful; you might want to draw upon this thread from the past and have lots of friends accompany you down the aisle. Or, in the case of a formal wedding, you may want to rely upon tradition: ushers down the aisle first in pairs, followed by bridesmaids also in pairs; then the maid and/or matron of honor, followed by the ring bearer, flower girl, and finally, the bride and her father. In the centuries-old Jewish ceremony, the bride and groom may be accompanied by both sets of parents, grandparents, or as many friends as they wish.

## · Music ·

T he strains of a musical prelude cue guests to the beginning of the ceremony. This prelude is anything from live music—organ, piano, violins, harps, flutes, or drums—to tapes of your favorite symphony orchestras or recording artists. The most traditional processional music is from Mendelssohn's "A Midsummer Night's Dream," written in 1826. This beloved music, now so identified with weddings, became popular in Europe after being played at the 1858 wedding of Queen Victoria's daughter, Princess Victoria, to Prince Frederick of Prussia. Queen Victoria's son and heir to the throne, Prince Edward, popularized another Victorian favorite at his 1863 wedding: Handel's Processional in G Major.

THE SINGERS OF THE CHOIR, THE SUBDUING
HARMONIES OF THE ORGAN, AND THE SWEETLY
MIRTHFUL RIOT OF THE BELFRY—
THE CLASH AND CLANG THAT TELL
THE JOY TO EVERY WANDERING BREEZE,

*John Cordy Jeaffreson*

## · W r i t i n g   Y o u r   O w n   V o w s ·

*T*oday, many couples wish to heighten the personal quality of their vows by writing part or all of their service themselves. Some use the traditional Protestant, Catholic, or Jewish ceremony as a format into which they weave the special prayers, poems, readings, and original thoughts that have great resonance for them. Others may wish to create an entirely new interfaith service that combines their own thoughts with elements of many religions. Still others plan to have their ceremony performed by a justice of the peace, customizing it to make it totally their own.

## · E x c h a n g i n g   V o w s ·

*T*his is an intensely personal part of the wedding ceremony. Here is where you can choose to recite the time-honored "I plight thee my troth," or create your own vows, drawing on the past. Whatever words you speak, they will bind you as surely as strands of reeds bound man and woman over two thousand years ago. You may not even need words at all, but actions, such as an authentic reenactment of a custom practiced in this country by couples of African descent over two hundred years ago. These enslaved people, denied their right to marry legally, would unite themselves to each other in a ceremony known as jumping the broom. There, in front of witnesses, the couple would act out their commitment by literally jumping over a broom together. Interestingly, this ceremony, known as a *besom* wedding, also took place in rural parts of Wales until the nineteenth century.

There are many resources available to inspire you. Happily, a wealth of literature is now within a bookshelf's reach, describing the ceremonial aspects of weddings from all major religious services and ethnic groups. Spend an afternoon or evening sharing a review of some of these with your mate-to-be. It will only deepen your wedding experience.

## · Wedding Bells ·

As the ceremony ends, the groom and bride kiss. This is truly one of the greatest of all wedding traditions. Just as the vow "I do" unites you spiritually, the kiss is the first moment in time when your bodies unite as husband and wife. Historically, the kiss has sealed the bargain.

Now, after the solemnity of the ceremony, it is time to celebrate. If your wedding took place in a church, you will most likely hear bells chiming. As you pull away, car horns will honk gaily. Why? Noisemaking is a time-honored way to chase away "demons." If you marry at home, it might be fun to supply your guests with horns, drums, and bells for this purpose.

*A kiss, when all is said, what is it? An oath that's given closer than before.*

EDMOND ROSTAND:
*Cyrano de Bergerac*

*Chapter Eleven*

# The Wedding Reception

THE GUESTS ARE MET, THE FEAST IS SET:
MAY'ST HEAR THE MERRY DIN.

*Samuel Taylor Coleridge:* "RIME OF THE ANCIENT MARINER"

hurch bells chime majestically. Fiddlers play merry tunes. The happy husband holds his bride's hand as bridesmaids and groomsmen, family members, and all the village folk follow. It's the procession to the wedding feast.

Cakes and ales are ready. Tables groan under the weight of meat pies, fruit tarts, and vegetable pasties, and excited children and dogs run ahead to steal as much food as possible. This jolly scene took place over and over in Europe from the Middle Ages on as weddings were celebrated with robust feasts that could last for many days.

Weddings are times to share food and drink with family, neighbors, and friends, and the tradition of feasting has continued unbroken throughout history. Early Greeks would feast with the bridal couple, then escort them home. In England, up until the eighteenth century, feasts were attended by the entire village, most of whom were so "overserved" that they slept over for the duration of the party. Wedding feasts were wild, bawdy events much adored by working folk, who needed them as a break from the harshness of everyday life. Merry revelers danced happily for days, ate extravagant amounts of food, and stretched the feast out as long as the food and drink lasted. Laws, as well as morals, were relaxed during the feast. The hard-playing guests had enormous fun with drinking contests, races, and athletic escapades. All across Europe this type of feasting was held. In Poland, peasants danced, ate, and drank, then worked for their hosts in exchange for this exuberant celebration.

Americans seemed to be spared this wild frolicking at their wedding parties. Most early settlers were a sober, hard-working lot used to enduring hardship. But they, too, loved to celebrate with dancing and feasting—although with much greater restraint. Many guests had to travel long distances, so the wedding became an opportunity for an extended visit, a prolonged family reunion.

In Europe, the tradition of exuberant feasting started to fade toward the end of the 1700s as the middle classes swelled and grew more prosperous. As most upwardly mobile people do, they tried to emulate the more sedate and sophisticated ways of the upper classes, who found uninhibited wedding frolicking to be unrefined. Over the next few decades, the feast was transformed into a one-day celebration, usually starting in the morning.

Prior to this, everyone in the community was expected to attend the wedding feast, having been invited by "bidders" who roamed the streets shouting out the particulars of the day and place. As gentility took hold, "crowd control" came into being. Invitations were delivered by servants or people hired for this purpose. Here, then, was the beginning of the written wedding invitation tradition, which has not only prevailed, but has turned into part of the vast wedding industry.

American society took its cues from the British. When wedding customs changed in Europe, they changed in the United States. Just as etiquette-conscious as the British, Victorian-era Americans absorbed new etiquette books with a passion. Isabella Mayson Beeton's *Book of Household Management*, published in 1861, instructed generations of brides in

*Love is sweet, but tastes best with bread.*

Yiddish proverb

the skills of holding the perfect wedding party. Elaborate, at-home wedding breakfasts and teas became the new tradition lasting well into this century.

Today, when most people think of a wedding reception, they think of an expensive meal held in a grand hotel or country club. How did the Victorian wedding breakfast become the reception? One theory is that a diminishing number of household servants after World War I made the at-home wedding difficult to stage. Another was that the upwardly mobile middle and upper-middle classes considered paying for a space to be an appropriate display of wealth. The rented space proved to have lasting appeal; now wedding receptions are a mainstay of the hotel and restaurant business. There is, however, an interesting reversal in this custom today, as more and more couples opt for the intimacy of marrying at home or in a place that has special resonance for them.

Whatever way you choose to celebrate—be it a wedding breakfast on the veranda of a lovely Victorian hotel, a cocktail party at a yacht club, a sophisticated midnight supper dance at a downtown hotel, or a picnic on trestle tables set in a leafy vineyard—there has been historical precedent for it. As you receive your guests, you'll be feeling the excitement of a festive tradition, sharing your bounty with friends and family.

# · Who Picks Up the Tab? ·

U p until the 1970s, it's been Dad. Wedding lore tells us that this long-standing tradition started with the first betrothals. The bride's father would celebrate his own good fortune in marrying off his daughter by inviting his friends and family to share in a meal. Naturally, he under-wrote all the costs associated with such a celebration. Soon, this evolved into a celebration for the couple themselves.

It is only in very recent times that this custom has altered. Today, the groom's parents or the bride and groom them-selves often share in wedding expenses. Some modern couples wish to circumnavigate the notion that the bride is still part of a property exchange. Others feel it is only fair to share. Whatever the reasons, the cost of the wedding can no longer be assumed to be the sole financial responsibility of the bride's family.

Weddings are expensive. How did couples celebrate if they had no money? In the past, communities would help. In England, during the Middle Ages, a custom began of holding wedding feasts called Bride Ales or Bride Bushes. This party raised money for the couple by charging admission, usually a penny or an enticing dish to add to the feast such as a pudding, meat pie, or sweet. A bush placed outside the party was the signal that all were welcome, even strangers, who usually found it hard to resist a wedding feast. Spread out over two or three days, these celebrations centered on the consumption of great quantities of ale or beer and were aptly named. Some see this as the forerunner of the community potluck dinner. It was really a kind way to help set up the new couple, who were given any leftover money.

## • The Receiving Line •

U sually, the first sight to greet excited and hungry guests upon entering the reception room is the receiving line. A fixture at larger weddings, the receiving line is a way of insuring that each guest is greeted, if only to exchange a few words. Often, the receiving line precedes the reception, but if the bride and groom wish, there can be one immediately following the ceremony, before guests move to the reception location.

The origin of the receiving line is credited to the change that occurred when weddings became more formal, invitation-only affairs at the end of the eighteenth century. Prior to that, wedding feasts had been wild free-for-alls with guests arriving at all hours. It was understandably difficult to know exactly who was in attendance at such a loose "open-house" gathering. Once wedding feasts toned down and required an invitation for admittance, all the guests arrived at about the same time, and it was considered courteous for the bridal party to be ready to receive them. Hence the term *receiving line.*

Bridal couples are often puzzled about who stands where on a receiving line. If you're planning one, remember: The only rules valid here are the rules of common sense, so arrange yourselves in the most comfortable way. If you wish to go by the book, the venerable Emily Post declares that the bride's mother should head the receiving line, and it is her duty to introduce guests to the groom's mother, who stands next to her. This stems from the days when the bride's parents were solely in charge of the wedding and acted as host and hostess. Any guests unknown to the bride's mother would, of course, be gracious enough to introduce themselves to her before moving down the line. The bridal couple stand next to the groom's mother, the bride to the right of the groom, so she may introduce guests to her new husband (the bride is an extension of the hosts and is expected to perform this social nicety). To the groom's left is the maid of honor and all the bridesmaids. For some reason, the fathers of the couple have been given the option of joining the receiving line or not—although Mrs. Post advises that if one does,

*Time flies,*
*Suns rise*
*And shadows fall.*
*Let time go by.*
*Love is forever over*
*all.*

ANONYMOUS

both should. Otherwise, they are free to circulate, collecting congratulations and quaffing champagne.

## •Seating Arrangements•

Some brides are intimidated by the idea of making a seating plan, fearing that they'll make a mistake. Not so. You don't have to be an expert in protocol to make a seating arrangement that's pleasing to all. That's because there are as many opinions about this as there are etiquette books. The *Complete Book of Wedding Etiquette* advises that the groom's family and friends sit on his right, and the bride's to her left, ending with her father. It is apparently an old custom to seat honored guests on the host's right. Traditionally, on the wedding day, the bride's parents were the hosts, and all who were to their right, including the groom, were honored guests. Emily Post sees this differently, however. She suggests the bride may sit to the groom's right with the best man next to her. The maid of honor sits to the left of the groom. The parents of the bride and groom would be seated at a specially designated parents' table along with clergy and honored guests.

Ultimately, the only guide you should have this day is your own inner voice. Seat everyone where they will be the most comfortable and near congenial company. Then you should relax because, at a wedding, goodwill is always the order of the day.

## • *Traditional Wedding Fare* •

*A*s guests arrive at the reception, attention turns to the wedding fare. First of all, it's a time-honored tradition to offer guests a drink. Wine has been the wedding drink of preference for the past two thousand years. The ancient Greeks and Romans saw wine as a symbol of fertility and provided copious amounts to guests. Britons drank a marriage mead; the Japanese serve sake.

When brides planned wedding menus in the past, they took care that foods offered were a reflection of the family's generosity. In the Middle Ages, the host of the wedding feast was expected to provide the best that his purse could afford—knowing that he would receive similar hospitality at other weddings. This custom was as true for peasants as it was for noblemen. In the thirteenth century, women would gather for days before the wedding, preparing sumptuous dishes for the epic feast. No sooner were pies of lamb, beef, quail, and other game removed from large ovens then in went the breads, fruit tarts, and pies. As the steam from puddings filled the air, kegs of ale and barley beer were rolled in. The forerunner of the wedding cake, trays of hard biscuits waited to be given out to guests.

Lavish displays of food remained a wedding tradition even when feasts evolved from groaning sideboard buffets to multicourse formal meals served by servants in the eighteenth and nineteenth centuries. The Victorian era saw the megacalorie meal in everyday life; wedding feasts were a special challenge in culinary stamina. Influenced by the sedate, sit-down wedding breakfasts of British royalty starting with Queen Victoria in 1840, the wedding reception was anything from a breakfast to a tea, dinner, or ball. Menus varied accordingly, but what they all had in common—and share with their predecessors—was a staggering amount and variety of food.

The great wave of ethnic diversity spilling onto America's shores in the nineteenth and twentieth centuries produced wonderful new foods for America's palate. Many wedding feasts featured beloved delicacies from the "old country" presented with the same pride and grandeur as solid American fare such as oysters Rockefeller and roast pheasant.

At the 1906 White House wedding of President Theodore Roosevelt's daughter, Alice, two breakfasts were held: one, an intimate gathering just for the bridal party, featured salads, pâtés, sandwiches, strawberries, grapes, ice cream hearts, and cake; the other group, a somewhat larger list of seven hundred guests, enjoyed an eleborate breakfast with President and Mrs. Roosevelt in the Blue Room.

British royalty has long loved the wedding breakfast concept. At her 1973 marriage, Princess Anne had a relatively small reception with one hundred thirty guests. They were served eggs, lobster salad, partridge, and as a common touch, onion and bacon rolls.

If you're thinking of having a wedding breakfast, perhaps you would like to include some dishes from a typical Victorian-era breakfast: Start with a fish soup, move on to an assortment of game and fowl, fish salads, pâtés, cheeses, cakes, cookies, and bonbons—all washed down with punches, white wines such as sauternes, Madeira, and champagne!

Formal dinners of the time consisted of at least six or more courses and offered an evening's delight to the etiquette devotee forced to navigate a maze of exotic silverware and china. Hardly vegetarian, these menus relied heavily on meat and game and took hours to serve and consume. This tradition of the long-lasting dinner is still robust today.

## ·The Toast·

LET US TOAST TO THE HEALTH OF THE BRIDE;

LET US TOAST TO THE HEALTH OF THE GROOM;

LET US TOAST TO THE PERSON THAT TIED;

LET US TOAST TO EVERY GUEST IN THE ROOM.

*Anonymous*

*I*f a wedding feast took place in the Middle Ages, the traditional accompaniment was beer or ale. Peasants could rarely afford wine; that luxury was left to the nobility. Once champagne was invented by the monk Dom Pérignon in the 1600s, it was as natural at weddings as caviar on toast. Fantastically festive, champagne ignites every sense. One of the most moving moments of the reception is the courtly tradition of the champagne toast to the bride.

How did the toast come about? One theory is that in sixteenth-century France, it was the custom for men to drink to the health of any ladies present; this evolved into wishing the bride well before the wedding feast began. Another part of wedding lore tells us that the wine-loving French would put a small piece of bread or "toast" on the bottom of a wine goblet to soak up any sediment the wine might contain. The glass was passed from lady to lady, each taking a drink.

The last to drink got the "toast," which was considered good luck.

An ancient superstition surrounding toasts is that they can be effective in chasing away evil spirits. Jealous spirits, always present at happy occasions, had to be outfoxed, especially at weddings. A handy excuse for more drinking was the belief that the clinking of glasses would scare off these spirits, who were reputed to detest loud noises.

One of the earliest recorded toasts was at the wedding feast of Rowena, the daughter of the Saxon king Hengist. Married in A.D. 450 to the British king Vortigern, this happy bride very graciously raised her goblet to toast her new husband with the tender wish, "Long, King, be of health."

While today the best man is expected to deliver the first toast, this is a relatively recent custom when we look back through time. Up until the beginning of this century, it was the bride's father who rose to his feet, glass in hand, to request that all drink to the health of his daughter. More democratically today, the bridal couple is toasted together, and the groom then stands in reply to say a few heartfelt words about his new wife. The bride remains seated as all raise their glasses to her. Then, any guest who wishes to may make a toast to the happy couple.

# · The Wedding Cake ·

WITH THE PHANT'SIES OF HEY-TROLL,
TROLL AROUND THE BRIDAL BOWL,
AND DIVIDE THE BRIDE-CAKE,
ROUND ABOUT THE BRIDE'S STAKE.

*Ben Jonson*

What is it about a wedding cake that turns us all into excited children? Is it its beauty, its size, or the touching tradition of everyone's sharing something so associated with love? The wedding cake transcends mere romance. It is the most recognizable icon of the feast and the emotional high point of the reception. Eating together is a strong tie, both to each other and to the past. Serving a special food from which all partake is one of the oldest rituals known to us.

As a symbol of fertility and plenty, the wedding cake is unsurpassed. But the wedding cake wasn't always a cake. If we look back to the days of the ancient Greeks, we see brides arranging piles of small hard biscuits to serve at their wedding feasts. These plain cakes were seasoned with sesame and sweetened with honey to symbolize the sweetness and bitterness of life, the "for better or for worse" concept of marriage.

It was hoped that these cakes could pass along the good fortune of the harvest to the bride and imbue her with similar success in childbearing. To help ensure such, little pieces from these cakes were crumpled over the bride's head. Indeed, this act may be the true origin of the tradition of throwing rice at the bride and groom, which is a modern variation on throwing grains at the couple.

The ancient Romans continued this tradition, adding their own stamp. At the wedding feasts of patrician families, brides and grooms observed the ceremony called the *confarreatio.* Small cakes made from grain (*far*), salt, and water were broken over the bride's head as a symbol of fruitfulness. It was considered good luck to catch a piece of this cake, and guests hoping to share in this plenty were urged to take home a small cake for themselves.

In the days of medieval wedding feasts, guests were offered baskets heaped with small dry biscuits. As cooking became more sophisticated and spices more available, the hard biscuit was softened to a spicy, richer bun. Heaped on a table in a great mound, these were urged upon departing guests. So many centuries ago, here was the antecedent of the modern-day tradition of giving away pieces of the "groom's cake" in small white boxes.

Wedding "cakes" remained in this form until the seventeenth century, when legend has it that a French chef traveling in England found it difficult to transport all those small cakes. He hit upon the idea of putting white sugar frosting on the cakes and stacking them. Voilà! They all stuck together and became the first true wedding cake, much like the French *croquembouche*, the airy cream-puff confection also dating from the seventeenth century, which still serves as the traditional French wedding cake.

The greatest wedding cake breakthrough of all took place in the 1800s after the discovery of baking powder, baking soda, and finely milled flours. These ingredients made possible light and airy layer cakes of great delicacy. Up until that time, "cakes" were more like fruit puddings—heavy, dark, and dense.

*I think we had the chief of all love's joys Only in knowing that we loved each other.*

GEORGE ELIOT:
*Spanish Gypsy*

These new ingredients were all that creative bakers needed. The demand for multilayered cakes with marzipan frosting or royal icing was nonstop. Swags, cupids, bows, and filigrees of icing swirled about the sides and tops of these light-as-air cakes, taking them to romantic heights never before seen. Growing in size and stature, the cake became the new centerpiece of the wedding feast. The modern wedding cake as we know it was born.

Queen Victoria's wedding cake was an apt example of the

extravagant spectacle the cake became. Weighing in at over three hundred pounds, it was nine feet in diameter and decorated with marzipan cupids and a statue of Britannia—in ice! Tucked inside were gold charms symbolizing love, an endearing nod to bridal tradition.

Royal weddings have always brought out the magnificent, at least as far as monarchs are concerned. In 1947, when England's Princess Elizabeth married Philip Mountbatten, their cake stood nine feet high and weighed five hundred pounds—a royal feat, especially in the days of postwar shortages.

It was the cake of Albert Edward, Victoria and Albert's son and heir to the throne, that started a new tradition—the custom of elevating each layer to make the cake even more grandiose. This was the beginning of all those towering edifices, although some cake historians think that the cake with columns came into being in the 1920s.

At the 1874 White House wedding of President Ulysses S. Grant's beautiful daughter Nellie to Algernon Sartoris, the bride and groom cut into a cake festooned with wedding bells, roses, and white doves. In our time, when Lady Diana Spencer married the prince of Wales in 1981, their cake was a five-tiered hexagonal shape topped with flowers. It was also a tradition at weddings of the upper classes in Britain to serve more than one wedding cake—a custom that has become established in America as well.

Nearly every civilization celebrates a feast with some form of sweet: The Iroquois Indians have a special cake of meal; Italians serve a delicious rum-soaked cream cake. Wedding cakes can be anything from mocha to carrot, hazelnut, chocolate, lemon, and almond. The eco-wedding, a new tradition-in-the-making, specializes in presenting only ecologically responsible food. If you were planning such a wedding feast, you would offer your guests a cake made of wholesome ingredients such as yogurt, instead of butter, egg whites without the yolks, and unboiled honey, instead of refined sugar.

## · T h e   G r o o m ' s   C a k e ·

*T*he sight of a tray piled high with tiny white boxes tied with lovely satin ribbon is a charming tradition. These boxes contain pieces of the "groom's cake"—which was once called the "bride's cake." How did this turnabout happen? Formerly, the "bride's cake" was the official wedding pastry. Heavy, dark, fruit-filled, this cake was served plain or frosted with a white icing. Even as light layer cakes replaced this one, the bride still had a place in her heart for the old "bride's cake." And so it remained, now redubbed "groom's cake." It was an old custom while saying good-bye to guests to hand them small bits of the wedding cake to take home for good luck. Now, the "groom's cake" performs that function admirably.

Some brides still prefer to serve a fruit-based cake at their weddings. Lynda Bird Johnson did so at her White House wedding in 1967.

## · Wedding Cake Superstitions ·

We all know that the bride and groom cut and eat the first piece of cake together. Sharing food is a sign of love. At Hindu weddings, the couple eat from the same plate. In China, it's wine and honey that is shared. Jewish couples sip consecrated wine from the same cup when taking their vows. It was an old German custom to share soup from the same dish. The Navajos prepared a maize pudding for the bride and groom to share. The Japanese bride and groom drink sake from the same cup.

But why must the bride be the first to eat the cake? It's another fertility rite. Superstition has it that her fertility could be "cut into" if she does not cut the first piece of cake and eat it.

*Who ever loved that loved not at first sight?*

CHRISTOPHER MARLOWE:
*"Hero and Leander"*

Alternatively, a custom at wedding feasts during the Middle Ages in France and England was that of passing small slices of wedding cake through a ring before eating. It was thought that this combination of the symbol of marriage and the symbol of fertility would prove lucky.

One of the best-known wedding superstitions is the belief that a small piece of the wedding cake, tucked under a pillow, will bring good luck to a woman hoping to marry. Wrapped carefully in the left stocking (same side as the wedding ring), this lumpy little treasure was thought to induce dreams featuring the faces of future husbands.

## · D a n c i n g ·

I talians do the *tarantella;* Irish dance a jig; Scots do the Highland fling; Greeks join hands in a chain dance they call the *kalamatianos;* and the Jewish people dance circles around the bride and groom in their famous dance, the *hora.* What's a wedding without dancing?

Dancing and entertainment are traditions at weddings dating back as far as the feast itself. Every age had its dances, be they sedate minuets or high-spirited reels. Dancing was a large part of social life for our early settlers, and fiddlers were in great demand, especially at a wedding.

Dances done in a circle, such as the *hora*, symbolize eternity. But it's more emotion than symbolism that prevails at a reception when that sentimental moment arrives as the first waltz is played. This is Dad's moment. Or it used to be. Contrary to contemporary practice, it had been a long-standing tradition for the bride to take to the dance floor with her father for the first waltz. After a minute or two, the groom might join in with his mother.

As the reception wears on, the dancing takes on a deeper passion and energy. Jewish brides are lifted high in a chair by guests dancing the *mitzvah tantz* (blessing dance).

Before the existence of disc jockeys and masters of ceremonies, poets in the Middle Ages would recite a special poem called an *epithalamium*, written just for the wedding. The most famous is Spenser's immortal poem, which evokes all the romanticism of a sixteenth-century celebration:

> OPEN THE TEMPLE GATES UNTO MY LOVE,
> OPEN THEM WIDE THAT SHE MAY ENTER IN,
> AND ALL THE POSTS ADORN AS DOTH BEHOVE,
> AND ALL THE PILLARS DECK WITH GARLANDS TRIM,
> FOR TO RECEIVE THIS SAINT WITH HONOUR DUE,
> THAT COMETH INTO YOU.
>
> BRING HER UP TO THE HIGH ALTAR, THAT SHE MAY
> THE SACRED CEREMONIES THERE PARTAKE,

THE WHICH DO ENDLESS MATRIMONY MAKE;

AND LET THE ROARING ORGAN LOUDLY PLAY.

*Edmund Spenser:* "EPITHALAMION"

## · *Wedding Gifts* ·

*I*t's now commonplace at weddings to see the bride circulating from table to table, receiving best wishes from her guests, along with some promising fat white envelopes. Modern-day Italian weddings, as well as those of other ethnic groups, still carry on the tradition of the "bride's purse," a large, white-satin sack used to hold all those enticing gifts. No one needs X-ray vision to know that inside those envelopes are money gifts for the new couple.

Gift-giving is as old as the wedding itself. The earliest gifts were gifts of food: meat pies, spice cakes, breads, cheeses, wine, or ale. But certainly, the most consistent gift has been money or some form of currency. While money as a gift has gone in and out of fashion—with some influential etiquette experts considering it "the easy way out"—most brides and grooms manage to find a use for it.

Wedding gifts were a way of helping the couple set up their home. In medieval times, typical bridal gifts would of course be handmade: embroidered linens, baskets, dishes, brushes, stools, purses. The early Dutch always gave gifts for the house: candles, cooking equipment, brooms for the hearth. In Colonial America, handcrafted goods like linens and quilts were very desirable. One remarkable custom is attributed to the French, who, it is said, gave money to the bride's mother to invest for her daughter and son-in-law.

The wedding tradition that seems to be going the way of formal teatimes is that of displaying wedding gifts. This was done until after World War I, another instance of brides copying the ways of royalty, who always displayed their gifts. Perhaps this display was the reason why so many people made it a practice to send lavish wedding gifts of silver, crystal, and china to the bride's home.

Every day leading up to the wedding, an excited bride-to-be would unpack yet another crystal cruet set, pickle fork, or oyster dish. So swamped with duplicate gifts was she that some ingenious merchant saw both an opportunity to relieve her burden and increase his business. In 1901, the first wedding-gift registry was opened at China Hall in Rochester, Minnesota. Generations of brides have been unknowingly in this individual's debt ever since.

While wedding gifts may be lavish or practical, it seems that those that are the simplest are the most charming and memorable. Queen Elizabeth II received a wedding present of a lacy shawl, hand-knit by Mahatma Gandhi. And for the wedding of Nathaniel Hawthorne and Sara Peabody, their friend Henry David Thoreau planted a vegetable garden at their home in Concord, Massachusetts.

## · Wedding Favours ·

*I*t's long been a lovely custom for the bride and groom to give their guests a small gift or memento. Biscuits were the first wedding favours, along with fruit and nuts— especially almonds. Later, feasts saw spice buns being pressed upon departing guests.

In the romantic Elizabethan era, wedding favours turned into small corsages of flowers, tied prettily into knots with ribbons to symbolize the marriage "promise." Worn by men and women alike, these favours were usually presented at the church so that they could be enjoyed throughout the festivities, and many were worn for weeks afterward. At the weddings of royalty, favours would be tied with ribbons of gold or silver, exciting much attention.

Some noblemen were so enthusiastic about their matches that they gave guests fabulous favours: jewelry, gloves, scarves, and handkerchiefs embroidered with the bride's and groom's initials. It's not too great a stretch of the imagination to suppose that these were the ancient ancestors of that popular wedding souvenir—the printed matchbook and cocktail napkin.

Sugar-coated almonds have always figured prominently at Italian weddings. This bittersweet combination again evokes the give and take of life. Charming miniature bouquets of these nuts, sometimes known as Jordan almonds, are wrapped up in tulle and tied with ribbon. One bride we know had them made from the tulle that had been cut off when her veil was shortened before the wedding. Adding to the loveliness of this gesture was the fact that the favours were all handmade by the bride's aunt. It's always a particularly gracious moment when the bride and groom, basket in arm, circulate about the reception room, making sure each guest receives a wedding favour.

*Chapter Twelve*

# The Honeymoon and Happily Ever After

A FAVORITE DRESS FOR TRAVELING IS HELIOTROPE

CASHMERE WITH A BONNET TO MATCH.

*Harper's Bazaar,* 1883

omantic, lazy, and dreamy, the honeymoon has long been an important part of the wedding experience. A vacation unlike any other, the honeymoon often sets the tone for a lifetime of happiness—be it long, blissful days on sun-drenched beaches, an exotic railroad journey across the European countryside, a glamorous cruise in the Caribbean, or a getaway to a rustic family cabin. The honeymoon might also be an exciting adventure such as backpacking or a trip filled with humanitarian purpose such as volunteering in a developing country. The only hard part of a honeymoon should be trying to choose just one from all the thrilling possibilities.

But more than simply a spectacular vacation, the honeymoon is a journey that runs parallel to the bride and groom's own journey of transition into the married state. It bridges the emotional distance between the ceremony and the setting up of a home. After a hectic wedding, what more could a couple want than peaceful, soothing days just to themselves? But honeymoons haven't always been languorous and restful. Like other wedding traditions, they reinvent themselves from time to time to reflect the changing social scene. Since today most couples have shared intimacy well before marriage, the honeymoon is no longer the secluded, let's-get-acquainted period of marriage myth and legend. Today, it's more along the lines of a much-needed break before resuming work and family responsibilities.

To previous generations, the "wedding tour" or honeymoon was fraught with high expectations and mystery. Many brides went to the altar unprepared or unsure about what marriage held for them. So the honeymoon was more than a trip to Niagara Falls; it was the beginning of a new, physical experience as well as a new identity. Queen Victoria was not atypical in this regard. Her words, written in her journal on her wedding day, capture the joy she felt on her honeymoon:

> After looking about our rooms for a little while, I
> went and changed my gown, and then came back to
> his small sitting room where dearest Albert was
> sitting and playing; he had put on his Windsor
> coat; he took me on his knee, and kissed me and
> was so dear and kind.
>
> *Queen Victoria:*
> JOURNAL, *February 10, 1840*

As dear and kind as most husbands are today, they were not always so in the distant past—especially when the husband acquired his bride through capture, by stealing her away from her family tribe. This is how some wedding historians see the origin of the first "honeymoon"—a period of hiding out from the outraged kinsmen of the stolen bride. While the groom was waiting for family tempers to cool, or the bride's tribe to move on, the couple was considered married. Sometimes this lasted for a complete cycle of the moon, which was a way many ancient peoples marked time.

Folklore has another explanation for the honeymoon. This postmarital interval is said to stem from a custom practiced by ancient Germanic tribes. Immediately following the wedding, on every day for a period of thirty days, the new couple drank from a vessel containing mead laced with honey. (It's interesting that this is yet another example of the popular marital symbol of taking the bitter with the sweet.) This "month of honey" or "moon of honey" later became known as the honeymoon.

Whatever its exact origin, the honeymoon has maintained a firm place in the wedding experience. With the sixteenth-century notion of love as a legitimate motivation for marriage, the honeymoon took on tremendous romantic luster, lending it the cachet it still possesses today. Granted, not all marriages since that time were love matches, as they mostly are today, but as strict betrothal laws loosened, the love marriage bloomed. It was not until the late eighteenth century, however, that the honeymoon became an expected part of the wedding celebration.

*Love, all love of other sights controls, And makes one little room an everywhere.*

JOHN DONNE:
*"The Good Morrow"*

To the newly affluent, middle-class Victorians, the wedding tour was a way to exhibit status. The socially conscious Victorian groom carefully planned the wedding trip to combine seclusion with display. The more affluent the couple, the longer and more lavish the trip. Honeymoons could last whole summers; month-long trips were not uncommon. Big cities were popular destinations as was the seashore, and, of course, Niagara Falls. The "Grand Tour" usually meant traveling about the European continent for six months or more. A contemporary equivalent of that might be taking the Concorde over, streaking from capital to capital aboard *Le Train de Grand Vitesse*, and returning home in under two weeks, which in today's time market is an extravagant amount of time!

## · Bedding the Bride ·

MY TRUE LOVE HATH MY HEART, AND I HAVE HIS,
BY JUST EXCHANGE ONE FOR ANOTHER GIVEN:
I HOLD HIS DEAR AND MINE HE CANNOT MISS,
THERE NEVER WAS A BETTER BARGAIN DRIVEN:
MY TRUE LOVE HATH MY HEART AND I HAVE HIS.

HIS HEART IN ME KEEPS HIM AND ME IN ONE,
MY HEART IN HIM HIS THOUGHTS AND SENSES GUIDES:
HE LOVES MY HEART, AND ONCE IT WAS HIS OWN,
I CHERISH HIS BECAUSE IN ME IT BIDES:
MY TRUE LOVE HATH MY HEART, AND I HAVE HIS.

*Sir Philip Sidney:*
"MY TRUE LOVE HATH MY HEART"

*E*very newlywed worries about when the honeymoon ends—but when does it begin? Before the arrival of actual wedding trips, in the bygone days of betrothal and barter, it was the European custom for many brides and grooms to demonstrate their cohabitation. Some cultures went so far as to require visual proof of a bride's virginity, since such a state would have commanded a higher premium in the betrothal negotiations. Often this was satisfied by the sight of a sheet stained with the "bridal blood" rather than by direct observation of the wedding night. The greater the bridal price, however, or the more important the match, such as in the case of high royal alliances, the greater the need for evidence that the couple had consummated the marriage. Thus sprang up the curious custom of "bedding" the bride and groom, which lasted until the eighteenth century.

Escorted by groomsmen and bridesmaids, the hapless couple entered the richly decorated bridal chamber, where ribbons tied to bedposts symbolized the knot of marriage. A special drink called a sack-posset warmed the bridal couple as they were put into bed. In the presence of witnesses, nature was supposed to guide the newlyweds on the beginning of their new relationship.

With the passage of time, this custom changed into a rollicking free-for-all, with as many wedding guests as possible cramming into the space around the bridal bed. Modesty was thrown aside, along with stockings and garters, as the guests made a mad scramble to possess these trophies, which indicated then, as today, who would be the next to marry.

## • Candlelit Rooms •

*F*ire played a part in the honeymoon in ancient days, just as the popular fantasy of a candlelit honeymoon suite does today. The Romans escorted the bride to the bridal chamber by torchlight, then later tossed out the torch to wedding guests. At early Polish weddings, the bride went to a bedchamber that was laden with flowers; male guests would circle the room with candles to chase away the demons of darkness, and then the groom would enter.

*But there's nothing half
so sweet in life
As love's young dream.*

CLEMENT C. MOORE

## • The Garter Toss •

*A*s we have seen, wedding traditions are tenacious. One custom that has come down to us through countless weddings is the garter toss, which takes place at the reception, usually after several champagne toasts. The groom removes a satiny garter, worn by the bride for this purpose, and tosses it to unmarried male guests, who line up as expectantly as seals at feeding time. With the same intensity, they spring for the garter. Presumably, the lucky recipient will inherit some of the bride and groom's good fortune. If you plan to enact this scene, you may want to be extra-enlightened and wear two garters, just in case unmarried females should demand "equal time" to catch some good fortune.

## • W h o  P a y s  f o r  t h e  H o n e y m o o n ?  •

While obviously this question is decided on a case-by-case basis, today, many couples live together and share expenses before marriage. In the past, however, the wedding trip was the sole responsibility of the groom and/ or his family. This custom dates back to the distant days of marriage by betrothal, when a bride was a purchasable item acquired by a man. Since the groom assumed all financial obligation for his wife, he was expected to underwrite the wedding trip. In the early 1800s, this trip could include members of the wedding party, so we can see that a groom had to be rather well-off to afford such generosity. In Victorian times, affluent parents often made handsome gifts of wedding trips to their delighted offspring. Today, this is still a lovely and extravagant gesture.

## ·*The Morning Gift*·

*A*nother charming tradition from the past is the gift for the bride on the morning after the wedding night. This piece of jewelry or special trinket was meant to delight a new wife. Some wedding historians attribute the custom to the ancient Danes, others to the Germans. Whatever its true origin, gifts exchanged freely between a couple are one of the hallmarks of love, and one given at this time conveys extra meaning.

## ·*Anniversaries*·

*W*hat follows a wedding in years to come are anniversaries. While an anniversary can celebrate anything from the first time you made love to your first romantic dinner, wedding anniversaries are special. When you celebrate them, your wedding comes to life again. Just as birthdays are milestones to celebrate every year, so, too, does the wedding anniversary mark the passage and success of another year of marriage. Two of the most memorable are the Silver Anniversary, marking the twenty-fifth year, and the Golden Anniversary, celebrating the fiftieth. But the most romantic anniversary of all is probably your first. The excitement and freshness of the wedding is still alive, "the bloom is on the rose," and with goodwill and planning you have enjoyed a glorious first year. This is an occasion to celebrate privately. In later years, perhaps your children and grandchildren will help you celebrate. For this first one, however, plan an intimate meal or weekend alone.

Traditions exist for this part of the wedding experience, too. In the past, brides have often saved the top layer of the wedding cake for this occasion. Before freezers were invented, wedding cakes were dark, heavy, fruit cakes, so well laced with spirits and sealed with a rich marzipan frosting that they could last through many anniversaries. Nowadays, either the maid of honor or the bride's mother supervises the removal of a portion of the cake for preserving. If you think you would like to try this custom, be sure to seal the cake well, and don't be alarmed if you don't finish a whole slice— frozen foods don't really keep their taste much more than six months.

Anniversaries are associated with minerals, gems, and other materials that we give each other to celebrate. Here is a short list of the most significant and commonly linked duos:

1st    paper

5th    wood

10th    tin

| | |
|---|---|
| *11th* | *steel* |
| *12th* | *silk* |
| *13th* | *lace* |
| *14th* | *ivory* |
| *15th* | *crystal* |
| *20th* | *china* |
| *25th* | *silver* |
| *30th* | *pearl* |
| *35th* | *jade or coral* |
| *40th* | *ruby* |
| *45th* | *sapphire* |
| *50th* | *gold* |
| *55th* | *emerald* |
| *60th* | *diamond* |

A lovely way to celebrate your anniversary would be to share a special meal featuring one or two dishes from your wedding menu. Set the table with your best silver and china, and a bouquet that echoes your bridal arrangement. Then light the candles, and over a bottle of frosty champagne (same vintage as served at the reception), look at all the wonderful photographs of your wedding, honeymoon, and first year of wedded life. Reading aloud entries from journals you may have kept will only enhance the special feeling.

*Chapter Thirteen*

# Wedding Superstitions

POINT YOUR TOES TOWARD THE STREET,

TIE YOUR GARTERS AROUND YOUR FEET,

PIN YOUR STOCKINGS UNDER YOUR HEAD,

AND YOU'LL DREAM OF THE ONE

YOU ARE GOING TO WED.

*American folk rhyme*

uperstitions are among the most whimsical of
wedding traditions. Weddings abound with superstition. Some are well known, such as the
bride being carried over the threshold, or showers of rice
and old shoes. Others have become standard aspects of the
wedding tradition. For example, the clinking of champagne
glasses and the clamor of church bells originally were used

to scare off resentful spirits, but now are done out of tradition. While many of us laugh at superstition in general, when it comes to weddings, few take chances. It's far better to err on the side of caution and wear the famed "something blue" than to risk the slightest mishap on such an important day!

Going back to the dawning days of marriage, superstitions came about as a sort of early warning system. During this delicate period of change, which the ancients deemed risky, the alert bride and groom were always on the lookout for omens, inauspicious or otherwise. Experience taught them to associate good things with certain signals from nature and its cycles. Outwitting the bad omens and embracing the good ones, such as marrying after the harvest, provided the union with an extra blessing of fertility. Our ancient brethren saw fertility in flocks of birds flying overhead at a wedding, and prosperity if the marriage took place during an incoming tide.

Oddly enough, once marriage was declared an ecclesiastical sacrament in 1439, superstitions became even more prevalent. They were not always the benevolent and charming rituals they are now. Happily, today's wedding superstitions preoccupy us in a lighthearted way. Most are picturesque relics from the past, their exact origins lost in time. Some seem almost to make sense, while others are frivolous. But for every

*Superstition is the poetry of life.*

JOHANN WOLFGANG VON GOETHE:
*Literature und Sprache,*
No. 908

bride who hopes her marriage will be happy and long-lasting, here is a selection to incorporate or merely marvel at. And, in case you should encounter an elephant on the way to your ceremony, please, don't worry; it means extra good luck!

## · T h e   B r i d e ·

*F*rom your gown to the timing of your tears, the nuptial path is strewn with old saws and sayings.

**Gown:** Brides beware! For centuries, it's been thought to be bad luck to marry in yellow, the color of jealousy. Don't reach for green, either, even if you do plan to marry on Saint Patrick's Day; it's the color of envy.

Another old superstition maintains that the bride must always add the final stitchs to her gown herself—and just moments before the wedding. Why? She is ensuring that her happiness, like her gown, will not be "complete" until she marries. Even royals take this one seriously. When Princess Anne married Captain Mark Philips in 1973, she gave instructions to her dressmaker that the last few stitches of her gown were to remain undone until just before the wedding. Since the princess royal was divorced some years later, you can draw your own conclusions about the efficacy of this superstition.

And, should you find a small spider in your wedding gown, don't go crazy. The industrious spider represents money, and some could come your way.

**Gloves:** It is an old notion that a maid should marry with her hands bare, but a widow must wear gloves, lest the misfortune of the previous marriage "rub off" on her next.

**Handkerchief:** Why does a bride carry a small handkerchief? Not because it's a fashion statement. No, the bride must always take care to shed tears just before the groom kisses her. It's an old sentiment that tears cried before a wedding mean none after. It's worth trying.

The tradition-loving Victorians also had superstitions about household linens. They thought that linens should be embroidered with the bride's maiden initials only. To embroider them with her married initials was an ill-favored presumption that the marriage had already taken place.

**Dressing for the ceremony:** Another old superstition warns that it's tempting the fates for the bride to see her image by candlelight in a mirror before the ceremony.

*There is no fear in love; but perfect love casteth out fear.*

I JOHN 4:18

· G o i n g  t o  t h e  W e d d i n g ·

Good luck is thought to come to the bride who sees a toad, spider, dove, or lamb on her way to the church. In the unlikely event of meeting an elephant along the way, countryfolk in eighteenth-century Europe considered this a particularly lucky omen. If, however, a bride should meet a pig, she was advised to go back home and set out again lest her marriage be burdened with the undesirable characteristics associated with that particular barnyard animal.

In Great Britain, it's always been good luck for the bride to be kissed by a chimney sweep on her wedding day. This relates to the belief that the hearth is the center of the home. A chimney sweep, as one who cleans the chimney of ashes, has special powers. In addition to making the chimney safe for a fire, he also removes any harmful spirits that might be concealed there.

## · At the Wedding ·

Once at the house of worship, the bride must take care not to enter any gateway through which corpses might be brought. Following in the path of a dead one could bring an early demise to her wedded bliss.

Many ancient cultures feared touching the ground. The dead were buried there, and it was thought to harbor fiendish spirits. Precautions were taken to avoid such danger. In old Japan, brides arrayed themselves in sedan chairs and were carried to the ceremony. Once there, they walked across a red carpet laid out to the altar place. Some credit this as the origin of the "red carpet" treatment. In the English country-side before the advent of the stretch limo, brides walked to their weddings over a path strewn with grains and herbs. These served two purposes: the grains prevented their feet from touching the ground, and they served as a lovely symbol of the fertility wish for the happy couple.

**The Bride's Behavior:** There are many admonitions about dropping or breaking things. Foremost among them, a cautious bride will never break anything on her wedding day; to do so might break the love of her marriage.

**The Groom's Behavior:** A groom had to beware of dropping his hat, or worse yet, the wedding ring. This went for his best man as well.

## • After the Wedding •

**Wedding Bells:** The bell is an important symbol of the wedding. Crepe-paper bells decorate showers, and many a Victorian bride posed beneath a massive bell made of fresh flowers and paper frills. When President Grover Cleveland married his ward, Frances Folsom, in 1886, the delighted couple smiled for posterity beneath a bell of white chrysanthemums. But what does the bell represent? Noise. Our ancient ancestors believed that demons were scared off by loud sounds, so following a wedding ceremony, anything that could make a noise was used to create a tumultuous diversion.

## •Who Wears the Pants•

*I*t's always been important to establish who will be master of household finances. In ancient times, this was not done through joint checking accounts, but by the bride and groom trying to wrestle control at the ceremony. Immediately after the vows, the Welsh bride would quickly purchase something for herself, usually a trinket from a bridesmaid in on the scheme, so that she would be the one in charge of buying things.

In old Germany, couples literally vied for the "upper hand" right from the start. After the vows, each would attempt, while holding hands, to place a thumb atop the other's, or a foot above the new mate's foot. Greek couples also like to take on this challenge; the bride attempts to cover her new husband's foot in order to establish dominance. This might be an amusing ritual to introduce, and then afterward, share the signifigance of it with your spouse. Remember, forewarned is forearmed.

*Where love is concerned, too much is not even enough.*

PIERRE-AUGUSTIN DE
BEAUMARCHAIS:
*The Marriage of Figaro*

## · *Planning the Wedding* ·

*I*f you are planning a double wedding, you may want to think twice. Folklore has it that a double wedding could spell bad luck for one couple, because it's just too much happiness for evil demons to overlook. Also, if twins want to marry at the same time, plan carefully. In ages past, they would always select different churches for their nuptials.

## · *The Couple* ·

*O*ne of the most popular wedding superstitions dictates that a groom not see the bride until just before the ceremony. Why? Lore has it that bad luck can come their way if they lay eyes on each other, because they have glimpsed the future before it happened. They should avoid being photographed together before the wedding.

## · *Shoes* ·

*T*here seem to be more superstitions surrounding shoes than any other aspect of the wedding. Dating back to biblical times, shoes were seen as a badge of authority because they lifted a person off the ground, differentiating them from barefoot slaves and serfs. Shoes were also used as a way of sealing a bargain. A father would give his son-in-law a pair on the wedding day as a symbol of transferring authority over his daughter. Some Anglo-Saxon fathers gave their daughters a tap on the head with shoes just before the ceremony. While a lot of brides would object to that touch, we see a contemporary reenactment in the gaggle of old shoes dangling from the bumpers of the new couple's honeymoon getaway car.

The Swedish bride will leave the laces of her shoes untied in hopes of bearing children early. In old Russia, the bride pulled off her groom's shoes.

## · S u n s h i n e  o n  t h e  A l t a r  M a k e s ·
## Y o u  H a p p y

S unshine was considered nature's way of being there for you. The beneficent warmth of sunlight upon the altar as the nuptials are being performed is not only a beautiful sight—it's thought to be super good luck.

## • *Timing* •

*T*he superstitious couple avoids ever postponing the date of their wedding. Apart from risking a deposit on a reception room, you could postpone your good fortune.

## • *Charms* •

*O*ne of the oldest symbols of good luck is the horseshoe. It even plays a part at weddings. Farm folk once believed that a horseshoe, displayed outside the ceremony or reception, open side up, deterred the devil from entering.

## • *Tying the Knot* •

*I*f you thought the expression "tying the knot" meant putting a noose around your neck for life, you will be pleasantly surprised to learn its true origin. Knots have long symbolized unions—in particular, the union of marriage. The "true love knot" has passed from the ancient Danes to the cultures of northern England and Scotland.

From Shakespearean times on, the highly symbolic knot took the physical form of wedding favours given out to guests. The wealthier the marriage, the finer the ribbon from which the favour was made. In eighteenth-century England, favours of embroidered silver or gold ribbon were worn by wedding guests at royal functions. If an ancestor of yours was lucky enough to have been a guest at Queen Victoria's wedding to Prince Albert, he or she would have received a special favour of white satin ribbon tied with silver lace. Perhaps because no one could top that, wedding favours soon fell out of style for the sophisticated. However, they were still worn by servants and they decorated the ears of horses that pulled the wedding carriage. Royal patronage of knotted favours surfaced in post–World War II Britain. In the 1947 marriage of the future Queen Elizabeth II to Prince Philip, wedding favours of red, white, and blue ribbons made a proud reappearance.

## · C a r r y i n g   t h e   B r i d e   o v e r · the  T h r e s h o l d

*A*s mentioned earlier, one celebrated wedding tradition is actually the result of a very old superstition. A part of marriage lore in many cultures, carrying the bride over the threshold can be traced as far back as the ancient Romans. It was done as a precaution against the ever-worrisome demons that haunted doorways, waiting to ensnare happy couples. If the bride were to trip entering her new home, or her new "life," it would be an unfavorable omen. Another part of Roman superstition required the bride to partake of a morsel of her wedding cake at her new hearthside in order to become a full member of the family.

In Scotland, the first thing taken into the new home was a vessel of salt with which to scare off malevolent spirits. In that country, it was also bad luck if soot fell down a chimney as the bride and groom arrived at their new home.

In old Russia, straw was burned in the hearth of the home of newlyweds to flush out any bad spirits inhabiting the chimney. All doors and windows were closed to prevent witches from entering. Today, a candle or two would probably do the trick.

## ·A Dream Is a Wish Your· Heart Makes

*F*or unmarried women only: To dream of your future mate, here's a surefire method practiced by country lasses over two hundred years ago. Sleep with a mirror under your pillow, and count nine stars each night for nine nights.

Be sure to wear a nightgown inside out, and don't forget to rub your bedposts with lemon before retiring.

To discover his initials, soak shoelaces in water till limp, then throw them at a wall and read the initials that emerge.

To find any mate: Eat one hundred chicken gizzards at one sitting; wash them down with the whole heart of one chicken—raw, of course!

*Chapter Fourteen*

# New Traditions

y this point, we have seen that weddings are as etched with tradition as the words upon the finest hand-engraved invitations. Traditions enrich all celebrations. Sometimes they make us think about the seriousness of what we are doing, such as when we marry in the same church as our grandparents. Sometimes they take our mind from what we're doing by creating a playful distraction, such as when we toss a garter or bouquet. But there is something special about the resiliency of wedding traditions. There are wedding traditions that time cannot alter, such as the plain gold wedding band, the vows of commitment, the kiss to seal love's pledge. Then there are wedding traditions that mirror the changing social reality: the coed bridal shower; invitations from both the bride's and the groom's family; remarriages. Weddings have a magnetism all their own, and when tradition makeovers are called for, weddings are among the first to attract them.

The most notable new traditions-in-the-making echo the voices now clearly heard from the women's movement and from ethnic groups proud of their heritage. Some new traditions are actually revivals of old-fashioned ethnic customs, once nearly extinct, now taken out, polished, and shined as beautifully as Great-Grandma's gold locket. Harriet Cole's popular African-American wedding planner, *Jumping the Broom*, gives black couples a wealth of ways to celebrate their weddings with a historical touch.

*The love we give away is the only love we keep.*

ELBERT HUBBARD

Ethnic groups have also created other new forms of bridal celebrations by pairing two ceremonies or receptions, one traditional to their native land, the other an American-style event. For example, a Japanese bride may wish to honor her family. For her wedding ceremony at a temple, she dons the kimono and elaborate hairstyle of the timeless Shinto wedding, then later celebrates at her reception wearing a classic, white, princess gown.

The ever-evolving concepts of female and male equality make themselves evident in the ways couples present themselves during the wedding. No longer is the bride viewed as the "property" of her father transferrable through marriage to her groom. Thus the word *obey* and the query, "Who giveth away this bride?" are frequently deleted from the vows. Hand in hand with this thinking is the wish to include mothers in a more meaningful way. Nowadays, we see many couples escorted to their place of vows by teary-eyed mothers as well as fathers, as has been the practice in many beautiful Jewish weddings. Some grooms cross gender lines altogether and select a dear female friend or sister to be their "Best Woman," and many a first toast is spoken by the maid of honor.

## • Name Changes •

*W*hat's in a name? Just as the wedding band is an instant signal that the wearer is married, the adopted last name of the bride is also an outward sign of her new identity. Until the 1970s, it was the prevailing practice for all married women to discard their birth surname upon marriage and share with their husbands a common last name. This convention was one of the first to be scrutinized by the women's movement, as the historical significance of the "wife as property" hit home. Some women compromised by taking hyphenated last names, while other brides kept their maiden names.

If you are struggling with this name-change dilemma, why not regard this as an opportunity to adopt any name you want? This private decision is yours to make in the absence of pressure; brides are not disappointments to the women's movement if they append their husband's last name, nor are they bold pioneers if they strike a different path. The real challenge of the last name comes when there are children and grandchildren involved—when there may be two sets of hyphenated last names to be made into one.

## · D i v i s i o n   o f   E x p e n s e s ·

*I*n the past, if you were looking for a detailed list of who pays for what, most etiquette books would have had very specific lists of obligations. For any father of the bride inexperienced in this field, seeing all these expenses spelled out should take place only in the presence of a person proficient in CPR! But the sharing of expenses is a tradition that feels the winds of change, too. Many weddings are fairly elaborate productions; the average formal wedding today takes a year to plan and costs twenty thousand dollars.

In the past, the bride's father was responsible for nearly the whole thing, except for incidentals picked up by the groom. Nowadays, some parents still want to finance festivities for their daughters. But there is an awareness that the expense of a wedding is one of the big price tags of true equality—for both the bride and groom. Every wedding is different; there should be no hard-and-fast rules about finances. Sometimes, a groom's family wishes to contribute when a significant number of the guests are theirs; other times, the bride and groom are established in their careers and wish to lift this burden from their parents. Fairness and consideration for all are the principles in operation for such a momentous occasion as a wedding.

## · The Electronic Wedding ·

*T*he videotaped wedding is one of the most popular new traditions. While there is still a place of honor on the bookshelf and in our hearts for the wedding album, it is now supplemented by an electronic album. Increasingly, weddings are being recorded by professional companies hired for the purpose. If you're considering video, just be sure to get a lot of reliable advice about makeup, hairstyles, colors, and lighting. Plan to view at least three of the firm's tapes so you can see what went right at other videotaped weddings—and what went wrong. And, most important, have a preview of yourself in your wedding ensemble on tape, well before the wedding. Cameras have a way of changing appearances in a surprising way. Perhaps you want to lengthen your dress in the back, lose a few pounds, or wear your hair up to show off a beautiful neck. Of all the times in your life, this is the one when you have to look radiant all day long.

## · Creating Your Own · New Traditions

*I*f being on the cutting edge of tradition appeals to you, why not create your own new tradition? It's certainly something that would personalize your day and heighten your memories. Perhaps you could plant a tree on your wedding morning or take all the children in the family out for gigantic ice cream sundaes the afternoon before? A ride to the ceremony in a vintage automobile with your flower girl and ring bearer bouncing in the rumble seat would have great style. Why not pass out tiny clay pots of myrtle, ivy, or rosemary along with small boxes of groom's cake? For an extra-personal touch, you might want to consider having your photographer take pictures of you with each guest to be sent along with your thank-you notes.

You could start a tradition that's socially responsible as well. Clean out your closets and donate extra clothes and shoes to a good cause. One couple we know had a duplicate wedding cake delivered to a shelter where they volunteer. There are so many fun and inventive things you can do this day, and the best part is that you can pass them along to your children and grandchildren.

*Love is all we have,*
*the only way*
*That each can help*
*the other.*

EURIPIDES:

*Orestes*

# Chapter Fifteen

# Wedding Readings

THERE IS NO MORE LOVELY,

FRIENDLY, AND CHARMING A

RELATIONSHIP, COMMUNION, OR

COMPANY THAN A GOOD MARRIAGE.

*Martin Luther:*

TABLE TALK

eddings constantly inspire new traditions. One of the loveliest and most moving of these is the verbal tribute. Whether this takes the form of a solemn marriage credo, an unabashed declaration of love, or "private words addressed to you in public," as T. S. Eliot declared in "A Dedication to My Wife," they are words unlike any others. Be they spoken at the time of vows, at the reception, or whispered in a moment alone, this tribute is meant to express the profound feelings held for one's love and to describe the depth and breadth of commitment to the marriage.

While we all have our own private thoughts and varying abilities to express them, many choose to borrow the impassioned eloquence of the world's greatest poets and writers for this purpose. This may be something you would like to do. If so, here is a small gathering of poems, psalms, passages, and fragments that articulate the magnitude of love and marriage. Some you may recognize as long-cherished favorites, others will be new to you. Some may apply solely to the groom, others to the bride, many to you as a couple. Why not set aside a few minutes on a quiet weekend evening and peruse this treasury? You'll discover many ways to use these beautiful declarations: on invitations, wedding programs, party cards, interwoven with your vows, as toasts or entries in your personal wedding journal, or, best of all, to inspire your own voice in pen or in person.

## • Marriage Credos •

Love is patient, love is kind.
It does not envy, it does not boast,
it is not proud. It is not rude, it
is not self-seeking, it is not easily

angered, it keeps no records of wrongs.
Love does not delight in evil but rejoices
with the truth. It always protects, always
trusts, always hopes, always perseveres.

*1 Corinthians 13:4–8*


In true marriage lies
Nor equal, or unequal;
Each fulfills
Defect in each other, and always thought in
    thought,
Purpose in purpose, will in will, they grow
The single pure and perfect animal,
The two-cell'd beating, with one full stroke,
    Life.

*Alfred, Lord Tennyson:*
The Princess; A Medley


Marriage is the union of two divinities that a third
might be born on earth. It is the union of two souls
in a strong love for the abolishment of separateness.
It is that higher unity which fuses the separate
unities within the two spirits. It is the golden ring
within a chain whose beginning is a glance, and
whose ending is Eternity. It is the pure rain that
falls from an unblemished sky to fructify and bless
the fields of divine Nature.

*Kahlil Gibran:*
The Prophet

A contract of eternal bond of love,
Confirm'd by mutual joining of your hands,
Attested by the holy close of lips,
Strengthen'd by interchangement of your rings;
And all the ceremony of this compact
Sealed in my function, by my testimony.

*William Shakespeare:*
Twelfth Night

A happy marriage has in it all the pleasures of
friendships, all the enjoyments of sense and
reason—
and indeed all the sweets of life.

*Joseph Addison:*
Spectator

A good marriage is that in which each appoints the
other guardian of his solitude. Once the realization
is accepted that even between the closest human
beings infinite distances continue to exist, a
wonderful living side by side can grow up, if they
succeed in loving the distance between them which
makes it possible for each to see the other whole
and against a wide sky.

*Rainer Maria Rilke:*
Letters

What greater thing is there for two human souls
than to feel that they are joined for life—to
strengthen each other in all labor, to rest on each
other in all sorrow, to minister to each other in all
pain, to be one with each other in silent,
unspeakable memories at the moment of the last
parting.

*George Eliot*

## • The Steps of Marriage •

Fling the golden portals wide,
The Bridegroom comes to his promised Bride;
Draw the gold-stiff curtains aside,
Let them look on each other's face,
She in her meekness, he in his pride—
Day wears apace.

*Christina Rossetti*

How it is I know not; but there is no place like a
bed for confidential disclosures between friends.
Man and wife, they say, there open the very bottom
of their souls to each other; and some old couples
often lie and chat over old times till nearly morning.

*Herman Melville:*
MOBY DICK

There is nothing nobler or more admirable than
when two people who see eye to eye keep house as
man and wife, confounding their enemies and
delighting their friends.

*Homer:*
ODYSSEY

In the long years of life must they grow;
The man be more of a woman, she of man...
And so those twain, upon the skirts of Time,
Sit side by side, full-summ'd in all their
    powers,
Dispensing harvest, sowing the to-be,
Self-reverent each and reverencing each,
Distinct in individualities,
But like each other, ev'n as those who love
Then comes the statelier Eden back to men;
Then reign the world's great bridals, chaste
    and calm;
Then springs the crowning race of humankind.

*Alfred, Lord Tennyson*

# • *Passion's Promises* •

Come live with me, and be my love;
And we will all the pleasures prove
That valleys, groves, hills, and fields,
Woods, or steepy mountain yields.

And we will sit upon the rocks,
Seeing the shepherds feed their flocks,
By shallow rivers to whose falls
Melodious birds sing madrigals.

And I will make thee a bed of roses
And a thousand fragrant posies,
A cap of flowers, and a kirtle
Embroidered all with leaves of myrtle.

A gown made of the finest wool
Which from our pretty lambs we pull;
Fair lined slippers for the cold,
With buckles of purest gold.

A belt of straw and ivy buds,
With coral clasps and amber studs;
And if these pleasures may thee move,
Come live with me and be my love.

The shepherds' swains shall dance and sing
For they delight each May morning;
If these delights thy mind may move,
Then live with me and be my love.

*Christopher Marlowe:*
"THE PASSIONATE SHEPHERD TO HIS
LOVE"

You are my husband [or wife],
My feet shall run because of you.
My feet, dance because of you.
My heart shall beat because of you.

My eyes, see because of you.
My mind, think because of you.
And I shall love because of you.

*Eskimo love song*


Wild Nights—Wild Nights!
Were I with thee
Wild nights should be
Our luxury!

Futile—the Winds—
To a Heart in port—
Done with the Compass—
Done with the Chart!

Rowing in Eden—
Ah, the Sea!
Might I but moor—Tonight—
In Thee!

*Emily Dickinson*


For whither thou goest, I will go,
And whither thou lodgest, I will lodge,
Thy people shall be my people,
And thy God my God.
Where thou diest, will I die,
And there I will be buried.
The Lord do so to me, and more also,
If aught but death part thee and me.

*Ruth 1:16—17*

# ·When a Man Loves a Woman·

Whoso findeth a wife, findeth a good thing.

*Proverbs 18:22*

I want (who does not want?) a wife,
Affectionate and fair,
To solace all the woes of life,
And all its joys to share;
Of temper sweet, of yielding will,
Of firm yet paced mind,
With all my faults to love me still,
With sentiments refin'd.

*John Quincy Adams:*
"Man Wants But Little"

Nothing lovelier can be found
In woman than to study household good
And good works in her husband to promote.

*John Milton:*
Paradise Lost

When you are old and gray and full of sleep,
And nodding by the fire, take down this book,
and slowly read, and dream of the soft look
Your eyes once had, and of their shadows
    deep;

How many loved your moments of glad grace,
And loved your beauty with love false or true;
But one man loved the pilgrim soul in you,
And loved the sorrows of your changing face . . .

*William Butler Yeats:*
"WHEN YOU ARE OLD"


The Fountains mingle with the River
    And the Rivers with the Ocean,
The winds of Heaven mix for ever
    With a sweet emotion;
Nothing in the world is single;
    All things by a law divine
In one spirit meet and mingle.
    Why not I with thine?

See the mountains kiss high Heaven
    And the waves clasp one another;
No sister-flower would be forgiven
    If it disdained its brother,
And the sunlight clasps the earth
    And the moonbeams kiss the sea:
What is all this sweet work worth
    If thou kiss not me?

*Percy Bysshe Shelley:*
"LOVE'S PHILOSOPHY"

## • "Us" •

You and I
Have so much love,
That it
Burns like a fire,
In which we bake a lump of clay
Molded into a figure of you
And a figure of me.
Then we take both of them,
And break them into pieces,
And mix the pieces with water,
And mold again a figure of you,
And a figure of me.
I am in your clay.
You are in my clay.
In life we share a single quilt.
In death we will share one coffin.

*Kuan Tao-Sheng.*
"MARRIED LOVE"


'Tis the gift to be simple
'Tis the gift to be free
'Tis the gift to come down
Where we ought to be

And when we find ourselves
In the place just right

It will be in the valley
Of love and delight.

*Shaker hymn*


## · My Husband ·


If ever two were one, then surely we.
If ever man were loved by wife, then thee;
If ever wife was happy in a man,
Compare with me ye women if you can.
I prize thy love more than whole mines of
    gold,
Or all the riches that the East doth hold.
My love is such that rivers cannot quench,
Nor ought but love from thee, give
    recompence.
Thy love is such that I can no way repay,
The heavens reward thee manifold I pray.
Then while we live, in love let us so persever,
That when we live no more, we may live ever.

*Anne Bradstreet:*
"To My Dear and Loving Husband"


Already the 2nd day since our marriage; his love
and gentleness is beyond everything, and to kiss that
dear soft cheek, to press my lips to his, is heavenly

bliss. I feel a purer more unearthly feel than I ever did. Oh! was ever a woman so blessed as I am.

*Queen Victoria:*
JOURNAL, *February 12, 1840*

## · *Come Away* ·

The voice of my beloved!
    Look he comes,
Leaping upon the mountains,
    bounding over the hills.
My beloved is like a gazelle
    or a young stag.
Look, there he stands
    behind our wall,
Gazing in at the windows,
    looking through the lattice.
My beloved speaks and says to me:
    "Arise, my love, my fair one,
    and come away;
O my dove, in the clefts of the rock,
    In the covert of the cliff,
Let me see your face,
    let me hear your voice;
For your voice is sweet,
    and your face is lovely."
My beloved is mine and I am his;

Set me as a seal upon your heart,
   as a seal upon your arm;
For love is strong as death,
   passion fierce as the grave.
Its flashes are flashes of fire,
   a raging flame.
Many waters cannot quench love,
   neither can floods drown it.

*The Song of Songs*
*(Song of Solomon) 2:8–10*

The Owl and the Pussycat went to sea
   In a beautiful pea-green boat,
They took some honey, and plenty of money,
   Wrapped up in a five-pound note.
The Owl looked up to the stars above,
   And sang to a small guitar,
"O lovely Pussy! O Pussy, my love,
   What a beautiful Pussy you are,
   You are,
   You are!
What a beautiful Pussy you are!"

*Edward Lear:*
"The Owl and the Pussycat"

## · *The Soul of Love* ·

Let me not to the marriage of true minds
Admit impediments. Love is not love

Which alters when it alteration finds,
Or bends with the remover to remove:
O, no! it is an ever-fixed mark,
That looks on tempests, and is never shaken;
It is the star to every wandering bark,
Whose worth's unknown, although his height
   be taken.
Love's not Time's fool, though rosy lips and
   cheeks
Within his bending sickle's compass come;
Love alters not with his brief hours and weeks,
But bears it out even to the edge of doom.
     If this is error, and upon me prov'd,
     I never writ, nor no man ever lov'd.

*William Shakespeare.*
SONNET CXVI


How do I love thee? Let me count the ways.
I love thee to the depth and breadth and
   height
My soul can reach, when feeling out of sight
For the ends of Being and ideal Grace.
I love thee to the level of everyday's
Most quiet need, by sun and candlelight.
I love thee freely, as men strive for Right;
I love thee purely, as they turn from Praise.
I love thee with the passion put to use
In my old griefs, and with my childhood's
   faith.

I love thee with a love I seemed to lose
With my lost saints—I love thee with the
    breath,
Smiles, tears, of all my life!—and, if God
    choose,
I shall but love thee better after death.

*Elizabeth Barrett Browning:*
Sonnets from the Portuguese

The sunrise blooms and withers on the hill
Like any hillflower; and the noblest troth
Dies here to dust. Yet shall Heaven's promise
    clothe
Even yet these lovers who have cherished still
This test for love—in every kiss sealed fast
To feel the first kiss and forebode the last.

*Dante Gabriel Rossetti*

Give all to love;
Obey thy heart;
Friends, kindred, days,
Estate, good fame,
Plans, credit and the Muse,
Nothing refuse.

'Tis a brave master;
Let it have scope:
Follow it utterly,
Hope beyond hope:
High and more high

It dives into noon,
With wing unspent,
Untold intent;
But it is a god,
Knows its own path
And the outlets of the sky.

It was never for the mean;
It requireth courage stout.
Souls above doubt,
Valor unbending.
It will reward,
They shall return
More than they were,
And ever ascending.

> *Ralph Waldo Emerson:*
> "Give All to Love"

Two partners of a married life
I looked on those and thought of thee,
In vastness and in mystery.
And of my spirit as a wife.

These two—they dwelt with eye on eye,
Their hearts of old had beat in time
Their meetings made December June,
Their every parting was to die.

> *Alfred, Lord Tennyson:*
> "In Memoriam"

First, God's love
And next...the love of wedded souls

Which still presents to that mystery's
counterpart.

*Elizabeth Barrett Browning*

New love is the brightest, and long love is the
greatest; but revived love is the tenderest thing
known on earth.

*Thomas Hardy*

## · G o o d  A d v i c e ·

In marriage do thou be wise: prefer the person
before the money, virtue before beauty, the mind
before the body; then thou has a wife, a friend, a
companion, a second self.

*William Penn:*
SOME FRUITS OF SOLITUDE

To do good and communicate is the lover's grand
intention. It is the happiness of the other that
makes his own most intense gratification. It is not
possible to disentangle the different emotions, the
pride, humility, pity, and passion which are excited
by a look of happy love or an unexpected caress.
To make oneself beautiful ... to excel in talk ... is to
not only magnify one's self, but to offer the most
delicate homage at the same time. And it is in this

latter intention that they are done by lovers, for the essence of love is kindness; and, indeed, it may so be best defined as passionate kindness—kindness, so to speak, run mad and become importunate and violent.

*Robert Louis Stevenson*

## · T o a s t s ·

May you have many children,
And may they grow as mature in taste,
and healthy in color,
and as sought after
as the contents of this glass.

*Old Irish toast*

May the wind be always at your back
May the road rise up to meet you.
May the sun shine warm on your face,
The rains fall soft on your fields.
Until we meet again, may the Lord
Hold you in the hollow of his hand.

*Irish blessing*

# Epilogue

*N*o matter what style of wedding is performed, a marriage unites two people into a unit unique unto itself. Whatever the accomplishments of that unit, be it a family dynasty, roots in a community, a thriving business or enterprise, the unit of the wife and husband begins as a fresh creation, as innocent and full of promise as any newborn. Traditions are guideposts that point the way to this new life: they are lanterns that illuminate dark corners; they are melodies that beckon one on to the right path. Traditions can be fun, such as tossing the bridal bouquet, or they can bring tears to the eyes, as when Grandmother's lace veil is donned.

Weddings are for optimists. We enter into them with the greatest goodwill we can bear for another person. And we hope that the traditions here deepen the beauty and joy of your most wonderful day.

# Bibliography

Bentley, Marguerite. *Wedding Etiquette Complete.* Philadelphia: John C. Winston Company, 1947.

Blayney, Molly Dolan. *Wedded Bliss.* New York: Abbeville Press, 1992.

Bloxham, Christine, and Mollie Picken. *Love and Marriage.* Great Britain: Webb and Bower, Ltd., 1990.

Brill, Mordecai L., Marlene Halpin, and William H. Genne. *Write Your Own Wedding.* New Brunswick, N.J.: New Century Publishers, Inc., 1985.

Brooke, Christopher. *The Medieval Idea of Marriage.* Oxford: Oxford University Press, 1989.

Coats, Alice M. *Flowers and Their Histories.* London: Pitman Publishing Corporation, 1956.

Cole, Harriet. *Jumping the Broom.* New York: Henry Holt Publishers, 1993.

Diamant, Anita. *The New Jewish Wedding.* New York: Summit Books, 1985.

Duke, Dennis, and Deborah Harding. *America's Glorious Quilts.* New York: Macmillan Publishing Company, 1987.

Eichler, Lillian. *The Customs of Mankind.* New York: Nelson Doubleday, Inc., 1924.

Fielding, William J. *Strange Customs of Courtship and Marriage.* Garden City, N.Y.: Garden City Books, 1960.

Ford, Charlotte. *Charlotte Ford's Etiquette.* New York: Clarkson Potter, 1988.

Fritts, Roger. *For As Long As We Both Shall Live.* New York: Avon Books, 1993.

Gies, Joseph, and Frances Gies. *Marriage and the Family in the Middle Ages.* New York: Harper and Row, 1987.

Glusker, David, and Peter Misner. *Words for Your Wedding.* New York: HarperCollins Publishers, 1986.

Goody, Jack. *The Culture of Flowers.* Great Britain: Cambridge University Press, 1993.

Karlin, Daniel. *Robert Browning & Elizabeth Barrett: The Courtship Correspondence.* Oxford: Oxford University Press, 1989.

Kelley, Leola Coombs. *How to Conduct a Perfect Wedding.* Philadelphia: Dorrance & Company, 1957.

Kirschenbaum, Howard, and Rockwell Stensrud. *The Wedding Book: Alternative Ways to Marriage.* New York: Seabury Press, 1974.

Lehner, Ernst, and Johanna Ernst. *Folklore and Symbolism of Flowers, Plants, and Trees.* New York City: Tudor Publishing Company, 1960.

Lockwood, Muller Georgene. *Your Victorian Wedding.* New York: Prentice-Hall General Reference, 1992.

Monserrat, Ann. *And The Bride Wore....* New York: Dodd, Mead & Company, 1973.

Munro, Eleanor. *Wedding Readings.* New York: Viking, 1989.

Nevill, Barry St. John. *Life at the Court of Queen Victoria.* Great Britain: Webb and Bower, 1984.

Northcote, Lady Rosalind. *The Book of Herb Lore.* New York: Dover Books, 1971.

O'Hara, Georgina. *The Bride's Book.* Great Britain: The Penguin Group, 1991.

Post, Elizabeth L. *Emily Post's Complete Book of Wedding Etiquette.* New York: HarperCollins Publishers, 1991.

Post, Elizabeth L. *Emily Post's Etiquette.* New York: Harper & Row, Publishers, 1984.

Reekie, Jennie. *The London Ritz Book of Weddings.* New York: William Morrow and Company, 1992.

Ross, Pat. *I Thee Wed.* New York: Viking Studio Books, 1991.

Rothman, Ellen K. *Hands and Hearts: A History of Courtship in America.* Cambridge, Mass: Harvard University Press, 1987.

Rubinstein, Helge, ed. *The Oxford Book of Marriage.* Oxford: Oxford University Press, 1990.

Schlereth, Thomas J. *Victorian America.* New York: HarperCollins Publishers, 1991.

Seligson, Marcia. *The Eternal Bliss Machine.* New York: William Morrow and Company, 1973.

Sitwell, Edith. *A Book of Flowers.* London: Macmillan & Co. Ltd, 1952.

Slater, Miriam. *Family Life in the Seventeenth Century.* London: Routledge & Kegan Paul, 1984.

St. Marie, Satenig, and Carolyn Flaherty. *Romantic Victorian Weddings.* New York: Dutton Studio Books, 1992.

Trevelyan, G. M. *English Social History.* London: Longmans, Green and Co., 1944.

Urlin, Ethel L. *A Short History of Marriage.* Detroit: Singing Tree Press, 1913.

Vanderbilt, Amy. *Amy Vanderbilt's Etiquette.* New York: Doubleday & Company, Inc., 1952.

Warwick, Christopher. *Two Centuries of Royal Weddings.* New York: Dodd, Mead & Company, 1980.

Woodham-Smith, Cecil. *Queen Victoria.* New York: Alfred A. Knopf, Inc., 1972.

# Index

Index